Building ON THE ROCK

A Biblical Vision of Being Church Together From an Anabaptist-Mennonite Perspective

D1210484

Walfred J. Fahrer

HERALD PRESS
Scottdale, Pennsylvania
Waterloo, Ontario

Library of Congress Cataloging-in-Publication Data
Fahrer, Walfred J., 1948-
    Building on the rock : a biblical vision of being church together
from an Anabaptist-Mennonite perspective / Walfred J. Fahrer.
        p. cm.
    Includes bibliographical references (p.).
    ISBN 0-8361-9001-7 (alk. paper)
    1. Church. 2. Mission of the church. 3. Church—Biblical
teaching. 4. Mennonites—Doctrines. I. Title.
BX8128.C55F36 1995
262'.097—dc20   94-48386
                                                                  CIP

The paper used in this publication is recycled and meets the minimum requirements of American National Standard for Information Sciences —Permanence of Paper for Printed Library Materials, ANSI Z39.48-1984.

Scripture quotations are used by permission, all rights reserved, and unless otherwise indicated are from the *New Revised Standard Version Bible*, copyright 1989, by the Division of Christian Education of the National Council of the Churches of Christ in the USA.

BUILDING ON THE ROCK
Copyright © 1995 by Herald Press, Scottdale, Pa. 15683
    Published simultaneously in Canada by Herald Press,
    Waterloo, Ont. N2L 6H7. All rights reserved
Library of Congress Catalog Number: 94-48386
International Standard Book Number: 0-8361-9001-7
Printed in the United States of America
Book design, cover, and inside illustrations by Merrill R. Miller

04 03 02 01 00 99 98 97 96 95 10 9 8 7 6 5 4 3 2 1

To the members of the Mission Commission
and to the staff
of the Indiana-Michigan Mennonite Conference
with whom I served
and without whom this book
would not have been written

Contents

Building on the Rock

"The believers church is coming into its own." Evidence for this statement by Wally Fahrer is emerging on many continents. In country after country, new congregations with an Anabaptist polity are being founded and are flourishing. At the same time, congregations from other church traditions, under the pressures of post-Christendom, are increasingly functioning like believers churches. The spread of the intentional church is symbolized by the increasing practice, by Christians in many traditions, of believers baptism.

But what is a believers church? Upon what theology is a believers church based? And how is a believers church structured? In a timely book for the third millennium, Wally Fahrer provides guidance for congregations seeking a coherent church life. Writing from the Anabaptist-Mennonite tradition and with careful attention to Scripture, Fahrer provides an inventory of building blocks for the construction of "primary, alternative communities of faith."

Fahrer is systematic in deploying his building materials. Foundational, he argues, is the person, life, and teaching of Jesus Christ. "Jesus is Lord and Savior": the church is built upon the rock of this voluntary confession made by each believer in the tradition of the apostle Peter. Growing out of Jesus' lordship and the disciples' intentionality are distinctive practices that equip Christian communities to flourish in an environment that does not provide incentives to the Christian belief or way. So Christians, building on the rock, will experience life-encompassing conversion. They will employ profound forms of initiation. Their understanding of Scriptures will be Christ-centered. And their approaches to many aspects of life—sharing wealth and counsel among members, developing leadership teams of servant leaders, responding to violence by "radical reliance upon the Holy Spirit"—will be both unconventional and hope-giving.

Fahrer's book is helpful because it is practical and accessible. In each of its short chapters, he deals with a significant area of congregational life in the Anabaptist tradition. Repeatedly he illustrates principles and gives concrete suggestions. Chapter-ending questions launch the reader into thought and discussion groups into fruitful give-and-take. I believe this book will be especially helpful for small groups, leadership teams attempting an inventory of the life of their church, and pioneer Christians trying to establish new congregations on solid foundations. it is significant, I think, that this book has emerged out of years of Fahrer's experience both as a pastor and also as an enabler of Christians founding new Anabaptist congregations. He pays tribute to the help which his comrades in these tasks have provided in the birthing of this book and thus indicates that he practices the mutual accountability which he so strongly advocates.

Wally Fahrer's style makes the reading interesting. He

writes clearly and simply; his illustrations rarely miss the bull's-eye; and his summarizing "common convictions" help to fix his message in the memory. He keeps a lively tone with colorful expressions, such as his contrast of "inspiration station" churches with "committed communities." On every page his faith and Christian experiences shine through. A Mennonite by adult choice and conviction, Fahrer's knowledge of other traditions and his charismatic and Evangelical experience give him deep resources to draw upon.

What will you gain from this book? Will it be its architectural analysis of the interlocking building blocks which together make a believers church? Or Fahrer's insistence that pastors are part of their congregations? Or that the church is called, not just to personal evangelism, but to "corporate evangelism" which offers to others the life of Jesus as expressed in the church's life together? For me, a sentence which summarizes Wally Fahrer's message is one that I will ponder and quote: "Our life together is our Gospel tract." As believers churches proliferate, I believe that *Building on the Rock* will help ensure that they are built wisely and well.

—*Alan Kreider*
Mennonite Board of Missions,
Overseas Worker
Manchester, England
14 January 1995

Unearthing the Treasure

Background

Building on the Rock originated with the Mission Commission of the Indiana-Michigan Mennonite Conference. I am deeply indebted to the members of that commission. They encouraged me and helped me put into words what I was groping to understand but did not quite see.

Our commission believed that God gave the Anabaptists a biblical vision of being church together. This vision, nurtured in Mennonite congregations, is a valuable gift which we offer to the Christian church everywhere.

As we began developing a strategy for a metropolitan church-planting initiative in the Detroit area, we faced a major obstacle: How do we start authentic Anabaptist-Mennonite congregations in an area basically unfamiliar with our denominations and their biblical understanding?

We soon decided that church planters should be trained in our core theological beliefs in order to found authentically Mennonite congregations that do not need to be ethnically Swiss-German or Dutch-German-Russian.

Mennonite Identity—Finding the Field

As we started to name core theological beliefs, we confronted a complicated issue: Mennonite identity. To unearth a treasure, we first had to find where to dig. We began to realize that Mennonite identity is a difficult issue to address. Mennonites are a part of a rich Christian tradition often referred to as "Anabaptist." This tradition is largely unknown or misunderstood. Yet it has impacted contemporary Christianity far more profoundly than most Christians recognize. Believers baptism, separation of church and state, voluntary church membership, freedom of conscience—all these are contributions of sixteenth-century Anabaptists and are adopted by much of contemporary Christianity. Yet at the beginning of the movement, such beliefs were punishable by torture and death, and thousands in Europe died for those convictions.

The name *Anabaptist* comes from two Latin words meaning to baptize again. It was a term of derision, assigned by their enemies, which has come to define a group of Christians representing what is often called the believers church movement. Most of those early believers referred to themselves simply as brothers and sisters. Sometimes called the radical Reformation, this movement of European Christianity was significantly and radically different from both Catholic and Protestant groups.

Although initially it had a profound impact on the lives of many people, spreading rapidly across Europe and into Britain, Anabaptist Christianity was largely silenced through persecution—but not from unbelievers! Those who claimed the name of Christ hunted down Anabaptists. Both Roman Catholic and Protestant governments persecuted the members of this movement, fearing the impact of their radical faith. Rejected by the mainstream of Christianity, Anabaptism was kept from fully becoming the instrument of spiritual renewal it might have been. Yet over the centuries, many church bodies embraced aspects of the vision the Anabaptists proclaimed.

These Anabaptist believers were forced to be refugees in country after country, to worship illegally in forests and caves or secretly in homes. They had no recourse to theological schools or denominational structures. Not until recently have their writings been more broadly available for study. Their lifestyle demonstrated their theology, and their vision was recorded in their actual life together.

Some of these Anabaptists became known as *Mennonites*, named after an early Dutch Anabaptist pastor and teacher, Menno Simons. The years of persecution and torture took their toll, and these believers became isolated and withdrawn. Today Mennonites are often regarded as a relic of the tradition they represent. Yet they have endured to see the vision for which they died begin to transform the character of the very groups who persecuted them.

Today we find at least three different meanings attached to the name *Mennonite.*

First, *Mennonite* refers to ethnic subculture(s). Individuals can be raised in this cultural community, choose not to follow Christ as Savior and Lord, and yet still call themselves Mennonite. This was not what we intended to describe or endorse.

A second use of *Mennonite* refers to denominational affiliation. Members of certain congregations identify themselves as Mennonites. Some of these groups may have moved significantly away from traditional Mennonite beliefs and practices while still carrying the Mennonite name. We were not interested in defining Mennonite merely in terms of organizational connection.

There is a third understanding of the name. *Mennonite* also refers to a unique set of beliefs and practices. Congregations may be part of a Mennonite denomination and still be out of harmony with Anabaptist-Mennonite beliefs and practices. Likewise, congregations outside a Mennonite denomination might be quite Mennonite in their beliefs and practices. On this set of beliefs and practices, we wanted to focus. We had found the field in which to dig.

Finding the Treasure—X Marks the Spot

While uncovering these unique beliefs and practices that characterize our Mennonite identity, we ran into a new problem: What is the *core* of our identity? We Mennonites do not describe our identity chiefly in terms of a code of common doctrines, as some denominations do. We have our confessions of faith, and yet we respect a variety of baptismal practices, understandings of end times, and expressions of worship.

Furthermore, we do not identify ourselves chiefly in relationship to a specific founding personality, as do some denominations. Although our name comes from an early Anabaptist leader, Menno Simons, we do not claim him either as founder or final shaper of our denominations. Neither our church history nor a common set of doctrines is at the core of our identity.

We began to understand that the heart of Mennonite identity is a common biblical understanding of being church. As Mennonites, our treasure is a unique vision of being church together. Thus our leading contribution to the world is our ecclesiology, our theological understandings of the church. Our identity is established more centrally around our practice of church than around either our written theology or our church history. To mark our treasure, we put a big X over our unique understanding of being church because it lies at the core of our identity.

Mennonite Ecclesiology—No Treasure Map

Jesus told a parable in which he described the kingdom of God as a treasure hidden in a field (Matt. 13:44).

Anabaptists have a treasure hidden in the field of their common life. It is a vision of church which has the stamp of the kingdom of God upon it. Even though its followers were horribly silenced, neither their work nor their vision is finished. I believe God has buried in the common life of these peace-loving people a vision to be preserved until the proper time. And it is their unique vision of church which lies at the core of Anabaptist identity.

When we asked what were the central understandings and practices of church, we discovered another problem. Mennonites have rarely written a simple definition of their ecclesiology! Protestants tend to describe their ecclesiology in terms of administering the sacraments and preaching the Word. But that would not suffice for a Mennonite understanding of church. To discover that required some reflection and study because we typically assume a common agreement and do not often try to articulate our style of being church.

What we discovered is that an authentic Anabaptist-Mennonite understanding of church is communicated more by experience and modeling than by spelling it out. In other words, it is more caught than taught. We needed to uncover the key characteristics of our identity—a unique understanding of being church together—which is at the core of who we are but has seldom been systematically defined or taught. In effect we had been looking for buried treasure without a map.

According to dictionaries, the common understanding of *church* in the wider culture is (1) a building for public, Christian worship; (2) that worship itself, as in "go to church"; (3) the clergy or officials of a religious body, and thus also a clerical profession; or (4) a body or organization of religious believers, which may mean the whole body of Christians, a denomination, or a congregation. These definitions overlook what is behind the word *church*. It comes from the Greek word for "belonging to the Lord" or "the Lord's" (1 Cor. 11:20; Rev. 1:10).

In Anabaptist-Mennonite circles, the first identifying characteristic of church is *community*. Church is more than a collection of individual believers who gather in the same building once a week for an hour or two. Rather, church is a recognized group of believers who share a common sense of *belonging to* the Lord Jesus Christ and to one another. This already moves us from the predominant understanding of church in our culture. Church is a *community of faith*. While this began to define our understanding of church, it did not go far enough.

The discovery of the second characteristic grew out of our attempt further to clarify the nature of this community. Church is not a religious version of a service club or a fraternal organization. It is distinctive, with a different value system. Its members consciously choose to live by the value system taught and modeled by Jesus Christ, as recorded in the Scriptures. The church is not just another community, but a genuine alternative to other societies. Therefore, we concluded that the *alternative* character of this faith community is a second identifying characteristic of an Anabaptist-Mennonite understanding of church. Church is an *alternative community of faith*.

As we began to describe this understanding of church, something still was missing. To Mennonites, this community is characterized by a sincere desire to follow Christ in life. Therefore, it has an alternative value system. But it also calls out a high level of mutual commitment and loyalty—a commitment even stronger than to one's biological family. Such primary commitment does not destroy other commitments, but challenges and transforms them. For Mennonites, a third aspect of our understanding of church is members holding to Christ in their primary and highest commitment. Our ecclesiology can be stated:

Church is a *primary, alternative community of faith.*

At last we could begin to unearth the treasure. The map had been recorded in the very life of Mennonite churches through history. To plant new churches and have them become authentic Anabaptist-Mennonite congregations, we needed to help church planters build primary, alternative communities of faith. This was our final task, to dig up the treasure and display it.

Unearthing the Treasure

Put another way, we asked ourselves, "What are the core themes or characteristics of such primary, alternative faith communities?" Our answers are the content of this study. It is our conviction that congregations reflecting these traits could truly identify themselves as Anabaptist-Mennonite congregations, no matter what ethnic identity or organizational affiliation they may claim. We are convinced that this vision is firmly based on Scripture and describes what God is calling every church to become, whether named Mennonite or not.

With the counsel of the Indiana-Michigan Mission Commission, I have attempted to communicate the essence of this faith community. Although I did not grow up in the Mennonite Church or in a Mennonite community, I have been a pastor in the Mennonite Church for more than twenty years. My wife and I joined a Mennonite congregation as adults. Yet despite our different backgrounds—or perhaps because of them—we have worked hard at understanding the unique identity of our faith family and communicating it to others.

What a Treasure!

Our experience has been one of unearthing a treasure in the midst of the field of the Anabaptist-Mennonite tradition and life. The treasure is a biblical vision of church which has excited us as we have worked at developing it.

Our study has gone through several drafts and was presented in a symposium format in February 1992. Since then, the material has been rewritten to accommodate a Sunday school or small-group format. Seven themes have become thirteen chapters, with discussion questions. I hope that as you study it together, you will discover the same treasure and will give yourself in fresh commitment to Jesus Christ and his church.

This Anabaptist vision of church has stirred something within me as I have worked at developing it. The more I have shared this treasure, the more convinced I have become that it is a vision whose time has come. As Mordecai said of Esther, "Perhaps you have come to royal dignity for just such a time as this" (Esther 4:14b). I have begun to feel that God has preserved this vision for just such a time.

In many areas of the world, God is restoring this vision —in part—to the church. Perhaps these are the new wineskins which God has prepared to contain the new wine of his Spirit. Over and over in the history of the church, the new wine of the Spirit has burst the wineskins of traditional Christianity. Unable to contain the work of God, the church has become rigid and reactionary, spoiling the renewal God was preparing. Perhaps this time we can learn and be ready. Perhaps this time we can become the people of God ready to impact the world for Christ.

—Wally Fahrer
February 1993
and June 1994

A Definition of Church

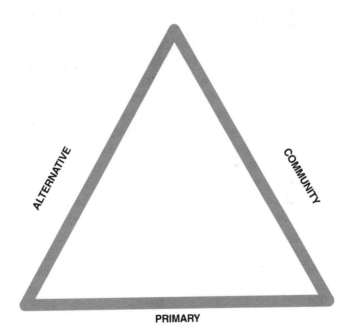

ALTERNATIVE

COMMUNITY

PRIMARY

CHAPTER ONE

Going on a Rock Hunt

Now when Jesus came into the district of Caesarea Philippi, he asked his disciples, "Who do people say that the Son of Man is?" And they said, "Some say John the Baptist, but others Elijah, and still others Jeremiah or one of the prophets." He said to them, "But who do you say that I am?" Simon Peter answered, "You are the Messiah, the Son of the living God." And Jesus answered him, "Blessed are you, Simon son of Jonah! For flesh and blood has not revealed this to you, but my Father in heaven. And I tell you, you are Peter, and on this rock I will build my church, and the gates of Hades will not prevail against it. I will give you the keys of the kingdom of heaven, and whatever you bind on earth will be bound in heaven, and whatever you loose on earth will be loosed in heaven." (Matt. 16:13-19)

Three Different Rocks
Rock No. 1: Peter Is the Rock
Laetentur Coeli, Roman Catholic Decree, 1439

We define that the Holy Apostolic See and the Roman Pontiff (the Pope) have primacy over the whole world, and that the same Roman Pontiff is the successor of Saint Peter prince of the Apostles, the True Vicar of Christ, the head of the Church.[1]

Rock No. 2: Jesus Is the Rock
Martin Luther, German Reformer, 1545

The Lord then says, "And I tell you, you are Peter, and on this rock will I build my church.". . . . Now the Lord wants to say, "You are Peter, that is, a man of rock. For you have recognized and named the right Man, who is the true rock, as Scripture names him, Christ. On this rock, that is, on me, Christ, I will build all of my Christendom."[2]

Rock No. 3: The True Confession Is the Rock
Pilgram Marpeck, Early German Anabaptist, 1542

On this testimony of Peter the new church of Jesus Christ was built . . . in accordance with the words of Christ when he says: "Upon this rock I will build my church or congregation" (Matthew 16:18). . . . Further, he says: "To this church I have committed the keys of heaven which forgives sins and retains them" (Matthew 16:19-20).[3]

Rocks or Gemstones?

In the southwestern part of the United States, there is a type of rock about the size and shape of a baseball. It is called a geode. On the outside it looks ordinary, even ugly. It is actually hollow, and when opened, it contains the most beautiful crystals. A geode is a real treasure for a rock collector. Not every rock is a geode. Most are simply rocks. But the joy of the hunt is to pick up a rock that is promising, cut it open, and find beautiful crystals inside.

The Christian church has been on a rock hunt for centuries. The treasure is hidden in the words of Jesus: "On this rock I will build my church, and the gates of Hades will not overcome it" (Matt. 16:18). The promise is that if we find the right rock, we will find Jesus building his church upon it. That certainly is a rock hunt worth undertaking. Unfortunately, not every rock is a geode, and not everything claimed to be the rock of Christ is the true rock of Christ.

Over the history of the church, different groups of Christians have offered varied identifications of the rock Jesus names in this passage. The Roman Catholic Church asserted that *Peter* is the rock of the church, and that the popes who followed him have been his successors. Hence, the true rock is that church which can be historically linked to Peter the apostle as its organizational founder—the Roman Catholic Church. The result has been an institution unequaled in our culture. But is it the true rock?

Protestants also have laid claim to this passage. They argue equally convincingly that *Jesus*, not Peter, is the true rock. Peter even said so in his first epistle (1 Pet. 2:4). Paul argues that "no one can lay any foundation other than the one already laid, which is Jesus Christ" (1 Cor. 3:11). So when Peter said Jesus was the Messiah, he declared the truth. This *understanding* of Jesus as the Messiah is the rock. By proclaiming this truth, the church will be built. The result has been a strong emphasis on doctrine. Correct doctrine ultimately became the foundation. But if that was Jesus' intended meaning, he certainly could have said it more simply. Is it the true rock?

Anabaptists picked up a third rock. Yet, in a way, it unites both of the other two. Anabaptists maintained that Peter's *confession* of Jesus is the rock. The difference may seem small, but it is significant. The church of Jesus is not built on a man (such as Peter), nor is it built on correct doctrine. It is built on the personal, voluntary confession of Jesus as Lord and Savior. That confession is part of what it means to be spiritually reborn.

Jesus invites Peter's confession with a personal question to his disciples: "Who do you say that I am?" (Matt.

16:15). Peter's response is a confession of faith in Jesus whom he had come to know as the true Messiah. Jesus' reply was all-important. He didn't say, "That's right! You get an *A* on your quiz." In fact, his emphasis was not on the answer but on the *source* of the answer. Jesus stressed that Peter's confession came from his Father in heaven. In effect, Jesus was saying, "This is a true confession; it has come as a revelation from God my Father, not from human sources. You have taken a step of faith. A new birth has occurred" (Matt. 16:17).

Jesus told Peter, "I will build my church on such confessions, for my church will be built on those who truly desire to follow me as their Lord" (Matt. 16:18). This is called a "believers church" understanding of the rock. Such a view of church is not primarily based on a historical tradition nor primarily on doctrinal orthodoxy. It is based, first and foremost, on personal transformation—a work of the Holy Spirit which allows men and women wholeheartedly to acknowledge Jesus as their Savior and Lord. Such a church may not be that attractive on the outside, but when the geode is opened, we find the crystals of true believers inside.

So the church is built on Christ, but not simply on a correct theological understanding about him. Jesus will build his church upon those who confess him as Lord, upon those who determine to follow him in life. In the same way, the church is also built on Peter. Peter was the first believer after Pentecost to invite both Jew and Gentile to put their trust in Jesus. He took the "keys of the kingdom"—the authority Jesus gave the church (Matt. 18:18; John 20:23)—to open the doors of the kingdom to those who truly confess Christ. Yet it is neither Peter's legacy nor the doctrinally correct statement which is the foundation of the church, but the genuine confession of faith in Jesus the Messiah.

First Keystone

No one denomination owns this understanding today. There are Catholic groups that are believer churches. There are Protestant congregations who call their members to publicly acknowledge their faith in Christ. And there are congregations in Mennonite denominations which function more like Protestant congregations than Anabaptist ones. A tradition, a denominational label, or history certainly does not guarantee faithfulness. The vision is bigger than any denomination. Jesus is committed to his church, not simply to a denomination.

In baptism, the assembly of believers still takes the keys of the kingdom, validates the confession of the new believer, and opens for him or her the doors to the kingdom of God. The members of the congregation believe the promise of Jesus, that what they bind on earth will be bound in heaven. They share a common conviction about the nature of the church of Jesus Christ:

We are closer to the vision of Jesus when we understand church as a community of believers who have voluntarily declared their faith in Christ as Lord.
The church is a faith community.

Jesus said he will build his church. This means he will continue to build his church according to his blueprint, whether or not we are a part of it. This means we have a choice. What kind of church do we want to be?

Discussion Questions

1. Explain in your own words the three different views of "the rock."
2. What view of church did you learn while growing up? Is it different from the one you hold today? Have you ever thought about the differences before?

3. How would you compare your congregation with the vision of church as a people who have "wholeheartedly acknowledged Jesus Christ as their Savior and Lord"? Is such a church possible?

4. What could your congregation do to strengthen this understanding of church as a community of people who acknowledge Jesus Christ as Lord?

CHAPTER TWO

Cathedrals or Caves?

For we are God's servants, working together; you are God's field, God's building.

According to the grace of God given to me, like a skilled master builder I laid a foundation, and someone else is building on it. Each builder must choose with care how to build on it. For no one can lay any foundation other than the one that has been laid; that foundation is Jesus Christ. Now if anyone builds on the foundation with gold, silver, precious stones, wood, hay, straw—the work of each builder will become visible, for the Day will disclose it, because it will be revealed with fire, and the fire will test what sort of work each has done. If what has been built on the foundation survives, the builder will receive a reward. If the work is burned up, the builder will suffer loss; the builder will be saved, but only as through fire.

Do you not know that you are God's temple and that God's Spirit dwells in you? If anyone destroys God's temple, God will destroy that person. For God's temple is holy, and you are that temple. (1 Cor. 3:9-17)

Looking Through Different Windows
Window No. 1: Church as Ceremony
Pope Pius XII, 1947

> The mystery of the most Holy Eucharist is the culmination and center of the Christian religion; it is the crowning act of the sacred liturgy.[4]

Window No. 2: Church as Proclamation Center
Martin Luther, German Reformer, 1580

> This is assembly of all believers among whom the gospel is preached in its purity and the holy sacraments are rightly administered according to the gospel.[5]

Window No. 3: Church as Community
Bernhard Rothmann, Early Anabaptist Theologian, 1534

> The true Christian congregation is a gathering, large or small, that is founded on Christ in the true confession of Christ. That means that it holds only to his words and seeks to fulfill his whole will and his commandments. A gathering thus constituted is truly a congregation of Christ.[6]

Worshiping in Cathedrals or Caves?

As a seven-year-old boy, I had the privilege of living with my parents in Germany for a year. Many times we visited beautiful cathedrals all over Europe. One of my outstanding memories was the sunlight streaming in through magnificent stained-glass windows. It was certainly one of the most visually beautiful experiences a boy could have! "Certainly God must be in a place like this," I thought.

Later I began to reflect on those experiences as I had the opportunity to take my own children to see some of the same cathedrals. I noticed all the gold on the altars, the hours and hours of painstaking work to cut and shape the stones, and the overwhelming size and cost of the structures. In my mind I compared them with the stories of early Anabaptists who were only able to meet secretly in caves. How different "church" must have felt, depending on whether one worshiped in a cathedral or in a cave! I realized that the perspective from which one looks affects the way one sees the object. In the same way, our perspective affects what we see when we read the Scriptures.

Our understanding of Scripture will change our perspective, and our perspective affects our understanding of Scripture. As an example, take the simple statement in Jesus' Sermon on the Plain: "But woe to you who are rich, for you have received your consolation" (Luke 6:24). Who are these rich? The average North American would probably reply, Someone like Donald Trump or the Rockefellers or Ross Perot. But if I were to ask the same question to a peasant farmer in Guatemala, I would get a much different response: The North Americans are the rich! Which reader is closer to the context of the authors of the New Testament? Most likely it is the peasant farmer.

The closer we can get to the perspective of the authors of the Scriptures, the more accurate will be our understanding of what the Holy Spirit wants to convey. The same principle applies to this study of church. Early Christians were a persecuted, illegal minority. Not until several centuries passed did the emperor Constantine favor Christianity and end the persecution. After that, the believer was no longer persecuted, nor a minority, nor illegal. There was one church, and it was a state church.

Centuries later, the perspective shifted again. With the beginnings of the Reformation, believers were caught between competing political territories. They were to have the same religion as their rulers, either Roman Catholic or Protestant. Princes chose the faith for their subjects. A person's faith was politically and geographically determined. So when early Anabaptists in Zurich, Switzerland, began to baptize one another as adult believers, they became an illegal, persecuted minority, as in the early church.

This change of perspective probably influenced the development of the Anabaptist movement far more profoundly than did the teachings of its founding leaders. With the decision to baptize one another came a profoundly new perspective on the Scriptures. These new believers found themselves in a setting like that of the early church. As a result, the Scriptures began to read differently. Rather than looking through stained-glass windows of cathedral Christianity, they were meeting in caves, reading the Scriptures in the shadow of suffering.

If the church is primarily centered on the holy ceremony of the mass, then it is assumed that it's the ceremony which God will primarily use to change lives. If one sins, one is to go to confession, receive the rite of absolution (after having done penance), and be forgiven. The central reason to gather as believers is to receive the sacraments. This was the predominant view for centuries.

With the Reformation, the emphasis changed. Preaching the Scriptures became more central. As the Reformation developed, depending strongly on the preaching of the Scriptures, so did the assumption that the Word changes lives. Nonetheless, one thing remained unchanged: What was done as a church centered on the special building and the Sunday morning event.

Through their experience of persecution, the early Anabaptists were not able to meet in a special building on Sunday morning. They had to meet in homes or barns or in the woods or in caves. As a result, their understanding of church began to change. They made a simple discovery: While the Holy Spirit has great ability to transform lives, they must first be yielded to Jesus Christ. Correct understanding of the Scriptures alone doesn't produce changed lives. First there must be a desire to obey the Lord. Until that time, no ceremony and no preaching ministry can change the heart. They began to see that real transformation of lives happens among committed believers.

Rather than seeing church as ceremony or as the center for proclaiming the Word, the Anabaptists started to live church as a community of committed believers. They were persecuted and no longer accepted by the society in which they lived. Thus they realized they could no longer depend on that society to shape their value system. Their church must take its cues primarily from the life and teachings of Jesus, as reflected in the New Testament.

Persecution drove these new believers from their homes and sometimes from their families. The Anabaptists began to consider the community of faith as their primary community, the one that took priority in their lives. They realized that no one else would be there for them if the church was not. This awareness further shaped their understanding of church. Rather than looking through stained-glass windows, they saw the church through the blood of the martyrs—and it took on a new meaning.

Second Keystone

The Sunday morning event is not what makes church. What makes church is the relationships of believers, God's "new creation" in Christ (2 Cor. 5:17-20). The church is a faith community, reconciled to God and to each other (Eph. 2:11-22). This conviction seems to be so obvious that we fail to appreciate its significance. Most of what we understand as Western Christianity has been shaped by the first two views of church. Although much has changed in the succeeding centuries, the instincts—the basic perspectives on the church—have been retained.

But within the history of the Anabaptist movement, a different view of church has been retained, a view important for our time. Neither culture nor government will continue to validate and affirm the church, so we are faced with a time of crisis for the state church. But the believers church is coming into its own. Once more, persecution and martyrdom are growing. In many nations, the church is again a persecuted, illegal, minority. Hence, we are led to the following conviction:

> We are closer to Jesus' vision of church when we see it as a faith community whose value system is shaped by the life and teachings of Jesus and whose relationships are characterized by a strong, loving commitment.
> *The church is a primary, alternative, faith community.*

Again, no denomination has a corner on the market when it comes to this vision. In many places, the church is no longer shaped by the value system of Jesus. It has become captive to the dominant culture and its values. In other settings, the church has become a secondary community or simply a valuable resource for individual faith. But where the church returns to the vision of Jesus, it begins to experience the power of the Holy Spirit once more transforming lives.

Discussion Questions

1. What would happen to your congregation if you could no longer meet together for public worship on Sunday mornings?
2. Put into your own words the three different views of how God changes lives.
3. With which view did you grow up? Is it different from what you believe today?
4. What could your congregation do to reaffirm that our value system comes from the Scriptures and not from worldly society?

An Understanding of Discipleship

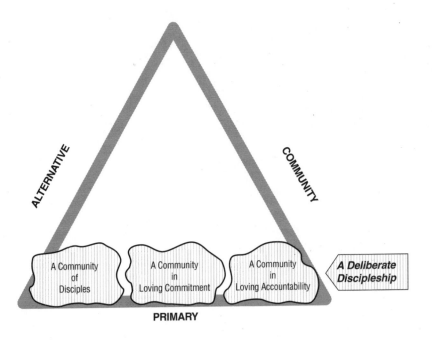

CHAPTER THREE

All That Glitters

As Jesus passed along the Sea of Galilee, he saw Simon and his brother Andrew casting a net into the sea—for they were fishermen. And Jesus said to them, "Follow me and I will make you fish for people." And immediately they left their nets and followed him. As he went a little farther, he saw James son of Zebedee and his brother John, who were in their boat mending the nets. Immediately he called them; and they left their father Zebedee in the boat with the hired men, and followed him. (Mark 1:16-20)

Witnesses from Mennonite History
Witness No. 1: Balthasar Hubmaier
Early Anabaptist Scholar, 1525

[The believer] is so minded, that he has already surrendered himself according to the Word, will, and rule of Christ to live henceforth for him, . . . and to allow himself to be baptized.[7]

Witness No. 2: Melchior Hoffman
Early Anabaptist Evangelist, 1530

[Believers should] also wed and bind themselves to the Lord Jesus Christ, publicly, through that true sign of the Covenant, the water bath and baptism.[8]

Witness No. 3: Menno Simons
Dutch Anabaptist Writer, 1539

In the spiritual strength which we have received, we henceforth bind ourselves by the outward sign of the covenant in water which is enjoined on all believers by Christ.[9]

Fool's Gold or Genuine?

There is an old proverb, "All that glitters is not gold." In fact, a convincing counterfeit is often called "fool's gold." Typically it is iron pyrite, a metal of little value that looks like gold. All prospectors have to know what they are looking for; otherwise they may be fooled by a counterfeit. The same thing is true with becoming a Christian.

My coming to Christ included a dramatic conversion experience (cf. Saul/Paul in Acts 9). There was a moment in time when a definite transformation occurred in my life. I was troubled when I came to know a number of believers who could not point to a specific conversion experience. They simply grew closer to Jesus over their childhood until they knew they were trusting him as Savior and Lord (cf. Timothy in 2 Tim. 1:5). The fruit of their lives—their daily walk of love for others and obedience to God—was ample evidence that God's Spirit was transforming them. At the same time, many of them felt like inferior believers when I spoke of my conversion experience.

Other believers I knew who had dramatic conversion experiences struggled after some years to keep the fire alive. They began to recognize problems that didn't go away despite their experience. Some of them searched for a second experience with the Holy Spirit. Those who could testify to such an experience freely acknowledged that not all of their problems left after the most dramatic encounters. A few began to look for a further experience.

As I reflected on what I was observing, I realized that many of my friends were on the quest for an "ultimate experience" with God. They were searching for a wonderful encounter with God—one that took all their problems away. Behind that quest was an expectation that they could find a transforming experience to sustain their commitment. They spoke of evangelism as leading someone to an "experience" of salvation. Thus they assumed that if one had such a dramatic experience, it would sustain a lasting biblical faith.

The longer I looked, the more it began to look like fool's gold. I began to see that such anticipation was similar to expecting the romantic side of courtship to keep a person faithful through the ups and downs of married life. Many assume that a high point of experience will sustain a commitment. However, the truth lies in the opposite direction. Lasting biblical faith is sustained by God's grace and by our commitment to follow Christ. Rather than looking for an experience to sustain a commitment, we must make a commitment to sustain an experience. This does not invalidate a dramatic conversion experience. On the contrary, it strengthens it.

There is, however, a difference between an initial encounter with Christ and a salvation "experience." I can still remember the first time I realized my wife loved me. It was the beginning of a relationship which led to our engagement, wedding, and married life. Those decisions were not based upon one experience. I did not expect the thrill of that initial experience—as wonderful as it was—to keep me faithful. Rather, the initial experience led to a commitment of faithfulness. When that commitment was made in public, I became a married man.

I began to realize the same was true in becoming a Christian. Instead of expecting a salvation experience to carry me and keep me faithful, I came to see that the experience is the beginning of a love relationship with Jesus Christ. When that love relationship leads me to make a public commitment to follow him and be true to his church, then I become a Christian. A commitment of faithfulness emerges from a growing love relationship!

This began to transform my understanding of baptism. Rather than baptism looking backward as a "symbol" that I have had a salvation experience, I began to see it much like a wedding service. In a wedding service, the bride and groom exchange vows of faithfulness to each other till death. They look forward to the life they will share together and publicly establish the foundation of their commitment. In baptism, I also declare my vows. Having come to know Christ and his forgiving love for me, I publicly declare my commitment to follow Christ in life.

If before my wedding, I had known all the changes that were going to be required in my life to make my marriage happy, I'm not sure I would have made that commitment. Nonetheless, from today's standpoint, I would gladly do it again. I think the same thing is true of being a Christian. I once heard a pastor say that in a time of prayer, he heard the Lord speak to him: "Bob, you and I are incompatible, . . . and I don't change." (Fortunately, my wife didn't take that approach with me.) Change is an essential factor of a faithful Christian life. We are to "grow up in every way . . . into Christ" (Eph. 4:15).

What sustained Sue and me through difficult times of change was not an initial experience of "falling in love," nor even an ongoing romantic relationship. What kept us together was a commitment of faithfulness, an allegiance rooted in our love for God and each other. The Christian life is much like that. It is a commitment to follow Jesus, an allegiance rooted in our love for him, which keeps us going through the difficult times.

Then I realized that just as a wedding involves two parties, so does baptism. As I publicly declare my vows of faithfulness to Jesus Christ, I am not the only one involved in that covenant. Christ also declares his vows to me. He promised he would never leave us or forsake us (Matt. 28:20; cf. Heb. 13:5). Our Lord seals that vow with a spiritual baptism. He gives us the Holy Spirit so that we have the spiritual enabling we need to remain faithful through it all. This is not the fool's gold of an ultimate experience, but the real gold of a genuine Christianity.

Discipleship is not simply an act of the will—a choice to follow Christ. The straight and narrow way is not a path I travel only in the strength of my inner determination. Just as married life is not simply a decision to be faithful, but a deep love relationship, so is discipleship. How good it is to hear those words "I love you," especially when I feel discouraged or defeated. In the same way, Jesus through the Spirit empowers us and encourages us in our walk of discipleship with affirmations of his love for us. This is the grace of discipleship.

Third Keystone

Becoming a Christian is much more than having an experience or accepting a specific list of doctrines. (We recognize that detailed doctrinal understanding is too great an expectation, especially of new believers from non-Christian backgrounds.) Rather, what is important is a commitment to follow—a commitment to learn and grow under the lordship of Christ. Here is the first characteristic of this vision of church: a voluntary allegiance to Christ as Lord.

Such a commitment must be based on a relationship rooted in the loving acceptance and forgiveness of Christ.

To begin otherwise is to go back to the bondage of legalism which has, from time to time, marred the history of the church. As Hans Denck, an early Anabaptist martyr, has said, "The medium [of discipleship] is Christ whom no one can truly know unless he follow him in his life, and no one may follow him unless he has first known him.[10] We share this common conviction about the nature of the church of Jesus Christ:

> We are closer to the vision of Jesus when we understand church as a people who share a common commitment to follow Christ in life. Rather than looking for an experience to sustain a commitment, we look for a commitment to sustain an experience.
> **The church is a community of disciples.**

Jesus called out, "Follow me," and his disciples left everything and followed him (Mark 1:16-20). They declared their commitment in water baptism and Jesus gave them a spiritual baptism in the Holy Spirit. From that band of disciples, the whole Christian movement has grown. Have you said "Yes" to his invitation to you?

Discussion Questions

1. How would you explain the difference between understanding conversion as an "initial encounter" and understanding it as a "salvation experience"?
2. What do you think is meant by thinking of baptism as a "backward-looking" experience rather than a "forward-looking" one?
3. Was your coming to faith the result of a dramatic experience or a progressive awareness of commitment?
4. Does your congregation understand conversion more as an experience to sustain a commitment or as a commitment to sustain an experience?

CHAPTER FOUR

A Rock Wall

*So when you are offering your gift at the altar, if you
remember that your brother or sister has something against
you, leave your gift there before the altar and go; first be
reconciled to your brother or sister, and then come and offer
your gift.* (Matt. 5:23-24)

Different Kinds of Stones

Type No. 1: Broken Stones

Everyone who falls on that stone will be broken to pieces;
and it will crush anyone on whom it falls. (Luke 20:18)

Type No. 2: Costly Stones

According to the grace of God given to me, like a skilled
master builder I laid a foundation, and someone else is
building on it. Each builder must choose with care how to
build on it. For no one can lay any foundation other than the
one that has been laid; that foundation is Jesus Christ. Now
if anyone builds on the foundation with gold, silver, precious stones, wood, hay, straw—the work of each builder
will become visible, for the Day will disclose it, because it

will be revealed with fire, and the fire will test what sort of work each has done. (1 Cor. 3:10-13)

Type No. 3: Living Stones

Come to him, a living stone, though rejected by mortals yet chosen and precious in God's sight, and like living stones, let yourselves be built into a spiritual house, to be a holy priesthood, to offer spiritual sacrifices acceptable to God through Jesus Christ. (1 Pet. 2:4-5)

Building a Rock Wall

I have always enjoyed watching skilled people doing their tasks, whether it be the woodworker making beautiful furniture, the potter making a graceful vase, or a painter creating a colorful scene on canvas. So I was excited when the stonemason arrived at our church meetinghouse to build a wall of natural stone. I watched intently as he picked through the supply of stones and began to lay the wall.

He carefully chose a variety of colors and shapes. Occasionally he broke a larger stone in two in order to fill a certain place in the wall. Between the stones was the mortar, holding all the stones together. The result was a wonderful wall with a variety of colorful stones which seemed to fit together well and yet were part of something much greater.

I incorporated the whole experience into my sermon the following Sunday. But even more significant, that scene began to be incorporated into my understanding of discipleship. When our invitation to faith begins with "God has a wonderful plan for your life," then it is easy to think that there is a plan with my name on it, just my shape, for me to fill. I had begun to think of discipleship as an individual undertaking. After watching the stonemason, I began to rethink that assumption.

I heard of a native Canadian community where the

children began to attend public school. The teacher, not a member of the tribe, asked the students to answer by raising their hands. One of the brighter students got the answers quickly, but instead of raising her hand, she whispered the answer to her classmates. When they all had the answer, they raised their hands together. In comparison with the teacher, they had a different cultural view of the role of the individual in community.

Jesus' view of the role of the individual within community differs from ours. When it comes to understanding Jesus' vision of church, our cultural individualism has become a real liability. The emphasis on self-fulfillment—my own needs and desires coming before those of others—works against the biblical view of the church as the community of believers. We tend to live with what I call the "myth of the individual victorious Christian life."

It came as a real eye-opener when I began to realize the false assumption I had accepted about Christian maturity. For fifteen years I had been a Christian before I realized I was trying to live a lie. I had thought that somehow Christians could reach a stage of maturity where they would have, in their own personal relationship with Christ, all the resources they would ever need to cope with all the crises of life. After that, if I had a crisis, my faith could always cope with it. I began to realize what a distortion that was. If I could reach such a state of maturity, I wouldn't need the church. I could be a Christian without the church.

I don't believe I am the only one to have this assumption. It has done much damage to the church. On the one hand, while things go fairly well, we assume we can do fine without the church. Then when things fall apart, we blame ourselves: Our faith should have been stronger. We should have prayed more. If we can't make it on our own, something must be wrong with our relationship with the Lord.

Behind that struggle is a faulty assumption that discipleship is an individual relationship with Jesus Christ. This is false. I began to see that the opposite was much closer to the truth. It is rare when individual Christians have all the resources in their own relationship with Jesus to cope with all the crises of life. That is why Jesus planned for the church.

When we try to be church with an individualistic view of discipleship, we don't see the need of community. If we are offended by a brother or sister, we just go on and leave our gift at the altar anyway (Matt. 5:23-24). If it gets really bad, we just stop going to the altar. But when we face the truth, we see the wisdom of Jesus in placing us with a community of faith. The reality is that *we need each other to live the Christian life.* When I am on top of things, I can help you back to strength. When you are up, you can help me stand. All of us lean on our relationship with the Lord. Discipleship is to be a shared experience within a community of faith. "Bear one another's burdens, and in this way you will fulfill the law of Christ" (Gal. 6:2).

Suppose I started telling you how much I want to be married and have children. Yet in the course of the conversation, I might let you know in no uncertain terms that I would have no relationships with women because I wanted to do it alone. You would think I was crazy, and you would be right. But when Christians talk about discipleship as an individual relationship with Christ, as following him through personal spiritual disciplines without being part of the faith community, they are just as crazy. We must be clear: You cannot be a disciple alone! Certainly there are instances when a believer has to stand alone, but those are the exceptions, not the rule.

Like the stones in the mason's wall, each of us stands as unique, but not in isolation. None of us is a wall by ourselves. We are only a wall together. Sometimes we must be broken and reshaped to fill the place in the wall that the mason intended. Our glory is not in being a beautiful stone, but in being a fitting part of the wall. Some stones may appear in places of prominence, but in isolation, they are not significant. Each believer is part of the greater plan of God for the church and ultimately for the earth. We together are God's holy temple, and God's Spirit dwells in us (1 Cor. 3:16-17).

Fourth Keystone

This means that part of our commitment to follow Christ, part of our baptismal covenant, is a commitment to be a believer "in community." Our society is rapidly losing the skills of being community. People in our culture are increasingly limited to superficial relationships because we don't know how to work through the hurts that intimacy produces. They expect the experience to sustain the commitment, so when the feelings change and hurts come, the commitment ends.

One of the essentials of community is commitment. Without it, there is no community. Jesus knew this, so he called for community, taught community, and modeled community. Only through an understanding of discipleship which is "in community" do we begin to glimpse what Jesus envisioned when he spoke of his church. Commitment does not just sustain experience, it sustains community. This experience of covenant community is a gracious gift of God.

The ability to make such a commitment to others is not as easy as it may sound. A simple determination to be there will not be enough. Instead, it is an empowering of the Holy Spirit. Paul said, "For in the one Spirit we were all baptized into one body" (1 Cor. 12:13). We might call it the grace of commitment. Therefore, we share this common conviction about the nature of the church of Jesus Christ:

We are closer to the vision of Jesus when we understand church as a community of disciples who share both a commitment to follow Christ and a commitment to love one another. These disciples experience the Holy Spirit enabling them to love each other despite hurts and disagreements.

The church is a community in loving commitment.

Discussion Questions

1. Can you identify with the sense of Christian maturity in which the individual believer is expected to stand all alone (the myth of the individual, victorious Christian life)?

2. Would you agree with the statement, "We need each other to live the Christian life"? How would that be true in your life?

3. How does your congregation work through the hurts that intimacy produces? Or do people leave when they are hurt?

4. How can your congregation embrace more fully the sense of discipleship happening "in community"?

CHAPTER FIVE

A Pile of Stones

I give you a new commandment, that you love one another. Just as I have loved you, you also should love one another. By this everyone will know that you are my disciples, if you have love for one another. (John 13:34-35)

Three Foundation Stones

Stone No. 1: Michael Sattler
Early Anabaptist Leader, 1527

> Further, dear fellow members in Christ, you should be admonished not to forget love, without which it is not possible that you be a Christian congregation. You know what love is through the testimony of Paul, our fellow brother.[11]

Stone No. 2: Ulrich Stadler
Early Hutterite Leader, 1537

> In brief, [the word] *one* [or] *common* builds the Lord's house and is pure; but *mine, thine, his,* [or] *own* divides the Lord's house and is impure.[12]

Stone No. 3: Dirk Philips
Dutch Anabaptist Leader, 1562

But how this came to pass, and how the building of the church of Jesus Christ was accomplished, the Scripture shows us with great clarity, namely, by the right teaching of the Word of God, by the faith that comes by the hearing of the Word of God (Rom. 10:18), and the enlightenment of the Holy Spirit.[13]

A Pile of Stones or a Building?

There is a big difference between a pile of stones and a building, just as there is a basic distinction between a collection of parts and an automobile. Gathering all the stones together in one place does not make a building, nor does getting all the parts together make a car. Some kind of purposeful assembly must occur before the one can become the other.

In the same way, there is an enormous difference between a collection of believers and a church. Getting believers all together in one place for an hour once a week does not make a church. Church is more than a gathering of believers. It is a community. As such, some kind of assembly is required. Somehow the individual parts need to be held together.

In response to the gospel of grace, the life of the believer begins with a commitment to follow Christ. Thus also the church as a community begins with a commitment. The essence of that commitment is to live in relationships of love with one another. Jesus said that the unbelieving world would know we are truly disciples by our relationships of love with one another (John 13:35). A community of love—that sounds like heaven on earth. Indeed! That's exactly what Jesus had in mind.

A major turning point occurred in our married life when Sue and I settled our commitment to each other. We had exchanged wedding vows, but when hurt and misunderstandings came into our relationship, we often responded, "*If* you really loved me, you wouldn't. . . ." At a Christian marriage retreat, we were both challenged by a speaker who encouraged us to settle our commitment. He encouraged us to tell each other, "I want to be the husband/wife to you that God wants me to be." Then he said we should affirm it in prayer and never question it again.

After that retreat, instead of saying, "*If* you really loved me, . . . ," we started saying, "I know you want to be the husband/wife to me that God wants you to be, so you need to know that what you did hurt me." The effect of that change was deep and profound. After several years of marriage, we finally began to build a foundation of trust under our marriage. I began to see how this was actually intended in wedding vows. We have called it a covenant of intentions.

Then I began to think of that principle as it related to the church. What is church membership to be? It is supposed to be a commitment of intentions to God and to one another. This commitment we make at baptism and renew in the Lord's Supper. Yet we are to live out and not just celebrate the "new covenant," based on Christ and the salvation he brings (1 Cor. 11:23-26). Instead of telling one another, "*If* you really loved me, you wouldn't . . . ," we can say, "I know that you wish to be the brother/sister God wants you to be to me, so you need to know that what you did hurt me."

For the church to become a community, we need to rediscover the biblical truth of covenant commitment within the body of Christ. It's one thing to be a fine automobile fender. But if I am going to be a part of a car, I need to let myself be attached to the other parts. That could mean welding and riveting. It could mean major change. In the church it could mean that a portion of my own individuality will have to be yielded up in order for me to be part of a community. Believers are like grains of wheat being ground to make bread, or grapes being crushed to make juice—a favorite early-church parable among the Anabaptists. As Christ suffered for us, we also suffer for each other in a fellowship of dedicated disciples (John 15:13; Col. 1:24; 1 Pet. 3:17-18).

This is a high price to pay in our culture, and many people are unwilling to pay it. Yet loneliness and isolation are the results of extreme individualism. However, a sense of belonging to others and knowing my life matters to them is more than worth the price. A commitment to become a part of such a disciplined community is at the heart of what it means to be church.

We need to be able to say that every member of our congregation has committed themselves to be the brother or sister that God wants them to be for one another. Those who are on our membership rolls are to be genuinely committed to being the community of faith with us and for us. That commitment lets us move from being a collection of individual believers to being a community of faith. That commitment provides the security and intimacy necessary to become a community. Knowing that you are committed to me and I to you, we can begin "speaking the truth in love" (Eph. 4:15). Of all the skills needed to become community, this is the most important.

Such a commitment means I am open to giving counsel and receiving counsel from the other members of my faith community. This flies in the face of the cry of our culture, "No one is going to tell me what to do!" Rebellion and defiance can kill community. Yet they constitute the spiritual climate of much of our Western culture. To begin to build community together, we need to communicate to others the importance of this openness to counsel.

When my fellow members in the body of Christ warn me that something is injurious to my spiritual health, I need to pay attention (Gal. 6:1). If they think what I am doing is jeopardizing my relationship with Jesus, I need to take their counsel seriously. Another word for this attitude is *accountability*. As an individual believer, my disobedience doesn't just reflect on me, but on my congregation and on the cause of Christ.

The scandalous behavior of some media ministers does not just reflect on their lives. All Christian ministry has been affected. The reputation of the Christian faith has been tarnished. This points out the need for accountability. Because my life reflects on my local church and on the cause of Christ, I need to be accountable for my behavior. Accountability is an important part of the loving commitment I make as part of the local congregation.

Becoming a building is more than simply piling up stones. It begins with a loving commitment and accountability to each other as individual stones. This is another characteristic of our vision of church. We are called to be a people of covenant, established through our commitments to love one another. The celebration of this life of commitment is the Lord's Supper. In the presence of the Lord Jesus Christ, and remembering the sacrifice of his own blood to redeem us to God, we reaffirm our unity and our love for one another. We are "living stones . . . [being] built into a spiritual house" (1 Pet. 2:5).

Fifth Keystone

At the end of this century, we are at a fork in the road between two views of church. Some regard the church chiefly as an "inspiration station." In this view, the church is organization and program, catering like a bazaar to varied individual interests, a full-service filling station. Others view the church as a "committed community." Anabaptist-Mennonites are most at home with this second view. But church as covenanting community is rapidly losing acceptance. Unless it can be embraced with fresh commitment, we are in danger of being swept along by the tide of popular opinion and practice.

The Holy Spirit is calling us to renew our vision. We can be a part of building vital faith communities! Such congregations will be characterized by relationships of trust and affirmation. Trust develops where the truth is spoken in love. Coercive authority isn't necessary when commitment is strong and alive. When commitment breaks down, traditions can substitute, and they may continue for some time. But real community is characterized by open and welcoming relationships. As believers, we share a common conviction about the nature of the church:

> We are closer to the vision of Jesus when we understand church as a community of disciples who have voluntarily committed themselves in loving accountability to God and to one another. We affirm our mutual desire to fulfill God's purpose for us to be brothers and sisters to one another.
> *The church is a community in loving accountability.*

With an Anabaptist understanding of the church, we are to be a church built on an understanding of discipleship lived out in community, a church built on a genuine commitment on the part of each member to love and care for one another, and a church built on mutual relationships of loving accountability. That is the vision to which we are called. We sense it as the call of the Holy Spirit.

Discussion Questions

1. What kind of commitment is required to move from being a collection of individual believers to becoming a community of faith?

2. Put in your own words the commitment to give and receive counsel from one another within the faith community.

3. What is the difference between the church as an "inspiration station" and the church as a "committed community"?

4. What could your congregation do to nurture relationships of loving accountability among its members?

A Model of
Authority

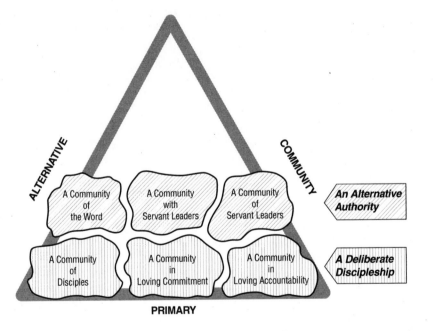

CHAPTER SIX

Whose Blueprints?

"Everyone then who hears these words of mine and acts on them will be like a wise man who built his house on rock. The rain fell, the floods came, and the winds blew and beat on that house, but it did not fall, because it had been founded on rock. And everyone who hears these words of mine and does not act on them will be like a foolish man who built his house on sand. The rain fell, and the floods came, and the winds blew and beat against that house, and it fell—and great was its fall!"

Now when Jesus had finished saying these things, the crowds were astounded at his teaching, for he taught them as one having authority, and not as their scribes.

(Matt. 7:24-29)

Understanding the Blueprints
Front View: The Product of a Master Architect

First of all you must understand this, that no prophecy of scripture is a matter of one's own interpretation, because no prophecy ever came by human will, but men and women moved by the Holy Spirit spoke from God. (2 Pet. 1:20-21)

Side View: Instructions for Proper Building

All scripture is inspired by God and is useful for teaching, for reproof, for correction, and for training in righteousness, so that everyone who belongs to God may be proficient, equipped for every good work. (2 Tim. 3:16-17)

Top View: An Accurate Representation of the Building

These Jews were more receptive than those in Thessalonica, for they welcomed the message very eagerly and examined the scriptures every day to see whether these things were so. Many of them therefore believed, including not a few Greek women and men of high standing. (Acts 17:11-12)

Building by the Blueprints

In a congregation I was pastoring, I remember counseling with a woman who was struggling with certain circumstances in her life. I asked if we could begin our time with prayer. As I was praying, I received a distinct mental image of this woman arguing with a contractor over which blueprints were to be used. The architect had supplied one set, but she preferred another. As I shared this image with her, she began to weep. She recognized that this image was exactly what was happening in her Christian life. She was able to talk through the conflict and submit her will to the Lord, and then she found peace.

When it comes to building a faith community, this same issue is significant. The question is, Whose blueprints shall we use? The role of the Scriptures is crucial when we get to this stage of the vision. It becomes a question of authority—which is a contemporary issue with potential for major conflict. In our age of individuality, we don't like anyone telling us what to do.

I discovered an interesting fact from raising my children. Youngsters have a great ability to misunderstand the

clearest commands when they don't want to obey them!
Yet they have a marvelous ability to understand what to do
in a confusing situation when they want to please and
obey their parents. I have concluded that the desire to
obey has direct bearing on the ability to understand.

When we examine the role of the Scriptures in the contemporary Christian church, we find real debate. Much
heat has been generated over questions of inspiration and
authority. While we should all be able to affirm these marvelous blueprints as products of the Master Architect, such
debate clouds a fundamental issue: An "orthodox" view of
the Scriptures does not ensure obedience to them.

A fundamental principle of the Reformation was that
preaching the Scriptures would produce changed lives.
The result was an emphasis on right understanding.
Preaching the Word became central to the worship of the
Protestant church. Doctrinal instruction became the focus
of Christian education. Creedal statements became tests of
orthodoxy. Proper catechetical instruction preceded
church membership.

Behind this way of being church was the assumption
that right understanding (orthodoxy) produces right
(righteous) living. While proper instruction does play a
key role, there is a basic flaw in that assumption. It has
been borne out over the years. Right understanding without the desire to obey does not produce right living. Rather, like my children, it produces all kinds of rationaliza-
tions and clever efforts to make the Scriptures say what we
want them to say. Right understanding does not always
produce right living (cf. James 4:17).

My own skepticism causes me to ask whether much of
what has been called biblical scholarship isn't rooted as
much in personal attempts to avoid obedience as in genuine scholarship. This is true, I fear, both on the conservative and on liberal sides of the issues. Those who teach an

"orthodox" view of the inspiration of the Scriptures are just as guilty of misinterpretation as those who teach a "liberal" view. For example, one justifies warfare from a conservative view of the Scriptures, and another justifies abortion from a liberal view.

In the midst of this maze, Anabaptists have traditionally held to a different emphasis. Rather than being satisfied with a stress on right understanding, they emphasized right living. The Scriptures, they argued, give directives for obedience, with God's help, not ideals that can't be lived. Issues of inspiration and infallibility are not as important as questions of interpretation and application. The key issue is not simply "What shall we believe?" That question is important but does not stand alone. We ask, "How shall we live out what we believe?" Blueprints are to help us know how to build.

Among Anabaptists, preaching was not a matter of one person having all the answers and telling the rest. Instead, it was declaring what the community of faith had come to believe as a faithful interpretation and application of Scripture. The congregation was to test the preacher's message (Acts 17:11; 1 Cor. 14:29). The faith community also gathers in small groups around the Scriptures to discover how to live. They discuss, pray, and seek the guidance of the Holy Spirit in applying the Bible to life. Larger groups of congregations together write confessions of faith as statements of current understandings of faithfulness to Jesus Christ, rather than systematic theologies or creeds.

Jesus said, "Everyone then who hears these words of mine and acts on them will be like a wise man who built his house on rock" (Matt. 7:24). Jesus' own life and teachings are the clearest example of the Christian way of life. They summarize the intent and meaning of all the rest of the Scripture. Christ fulfills the Old Testament (John 1:16-17; Heb. 1:1-4). Hence, all the commands and examples of the Old Testament ultimately yield priority to his life and teaching and saving work. The rest of the New Testament reflects on the Jesus event and applies it in new settings. This Christ-centered principle of interpretation also became fundamental to an Anabaptist understanding of the authority of the Scriptures.

The Scriptures reveal God's intention for the value system of the people of God. They were inspired by God and written by his people, for his people. Therefore, they are uniquely at home among his people. For the people of God, the surrounding culture should not dictate the value system of the faith community. Rather, the Scriptures determine our pattern of obedience, cutting across culture and reshaping it.

A basic Anabaptist principle of interpretation is known as the principle of obedience. An early Anabaptist, Bernhard Rothmann, wrote, "Thus God has restored the Scriptures among us. In them, his will is abundantly known to us, and we will adhere to them alone. And if we, with constant diligence, earnestly do what we understand, we will daily be taught further by God."[14] This means there are parts of the Scripture which we don't understand. But if we begin by obeying those parts we do understand, God will grant us greater understanding (John 7:17).

Unless we desire to obey God, no amount of correct theology will be profitable for the church. On the other hand, our obedience to the basic truths of Scripture opens the door to greater understanding of its intent and meaning. This became clear to me at a significant time in my life. It began as a deliberate attempt to obey the scriptural admonition to "give thanks in all circumstances, for this is the will of God in Christ Jesus for you" (1 Thess. 5:18).

The first result of my deliberate choice to give thanks was to see a change in my negative attitude. It began to diminish and disappear as I voiced what I sometimes did not believe. But the real breakthrough came somewhat later. At a crucial point of struggle and prayer, a Christian friend asked me if I had ever given thanks in the death of my parents. They had died years earlier, my father when I was twelve, and my mother when I was eighteen.

Tears of healing flowed from my eyes when I began to obey God's Word and gave God thanks in the midst of my loss. I discovered that thanksgiving opened a door to faith and healing. Rather than the pain and loss being a barrier to God's love, in giving thanks I began to believe in God's love through and beyond my pain and loss. The result was a new and deeper understanding of God's Word both emotionally and intellectually. What had seemed to be a difficult and uncaring command, was in reality a loving door to healing. Simple obedience led to deeper understanding and also to greater wholeness. Scriptures are meant to be lived.

Sixth Keystone

Mennonites have carried a tradition called "biblical nonconformity." This refers to a practice in which Christians take their value system from the teachings and example of Christ as revealed in the Scriptures, rather than from surrounding culture. In cultures where biblical values have had a pervasive influence, there may seem to be little difference between the church and the culture. But keep alert and "test everything" (1 Thess. 5:21)! In cultures where biblical values have not been honored, the church is obviously an alternative community. However, maintaining an alternative biblical community is not easy.

In the past, we have yielded too much to the temptation of withdrawing and isolating ourselves. We think, "As long as we don't have too much contact with the other value systems, we won't be seduced by them." However, we won't reach the world for Christ that way, and God loves the whole world (John 3:16). The other temptation is indiscriminate conformity to the larger society. This results in an inability to witness with integrity. Throughout history, the church has fallen off into the ditch on both sides of this road. Nonetheless, there is a fundamental Anabaptist-Mennonite conviction about the nature of church:

> We are closer to the vision of Jesus for the church when we approach the Scriptures with a commitment to obey them, especially as they are revealed in the life and teachings of Jesus. Kingdom authority is released in a community of faith which is committed to such an alternative value system.
> *The church is a community of the Word.*

This is another characteristic of Jesus' vision of church. Such congregations are characterized by the corporate reading of the Scriptures. We want to help each member to be a student of the Bible. To symbolize this understanding, an open Bible often lies in front of the congregation as it worships. Study of the Scriptures expresses our commitment to follow Christ in life. As a motto, it might be expressed this way: "Those who truly know Christ follow him through obedience to the Scriptures."

Discussion Questions

1. Do you agree that there is a direct connection between the desire to obey and the ability to understand?
2. What is wrong with the assumption that right doctrine produces right living?
3. Does the Bible serve as the standard for the value system of your congregation, or are believers more influenced by the surrounding culture?
4. How could your congregation encourage its members to build their lives around the blueprints of Scripture?

CHAPTER SEVEN

Who Are the Contractors?

A dispute also arose among them as to which one of them was to be regarded as the greatest. But he said to them, "The kings of the Gentiles lord it over them; and those in authority over them are called benefactors. But not so with you; rather the greatest among you must become like the youngest, and the leader like one who serves. For who is greater, the one who is at the table or the one who serves? Is it not the one at the table? But I am among you as one who serves.

"You are those who have stood by me in my trials; and I confer on you, just as my Father has conferred on me, a kingdom, so that you may eat and drink at my table in my kingdom, and you will sit on thrones judging the twelve tribes of Israel." (Luke 22:24-30)

Choosing the Contractors

Contractor No. 1: Michael Sattler
Early Anabaptist Leader, 1527

We have been united as follows concerning the shepherds in the church of God. The shepherd in the church shall . . .

read and exhort and teach, warn, admonish, or ban in the congregation and properly preside among the sisters and brothers in the prayer and in the breaking of bread, and in all things to take care of the body of Christ, that it may be built up and developed, so that the name of God might be praised and honored through us.[15]

Contractor No. 2: Hans Hotz
Anabaptist Spokesman, 1538

Concerning our calling and commission to the ministry of preaching we answer as follows. A Christian community . . . has the authority to send them to preach the gospel. [But] before there can be Christian preaching, there must first be a change of life, improvement, and the new birth. Then, if the virtues are detected in such a person, the commissioning follows as Christ called the apostles to follow him. . . . Only then he sent them and commanded them to preach the good news.[16]

Contractor No. 3: Peter Riedemann
Important Hutterite Leader, 1542

If the church needs one or, indeed, more ministers, she must not elect them as pleases herself, but wait upon the Lord to see whom he chooses and shows them. Therefore, they should continue in earnest prayer and petition to God that he might care for them, answer their need, and show them whom he has chosen for his ministry. . . . None, however, is confirmed in his office except he be first proved and revealed to the church, and have the testimony of a good life and walk.[17]

Who Chooses the Leaders?

In building the church according to the blueprints of Jesus, we come to a second critical question of authority: Who chooses the leaders? Like choosing contractors to build a building, choosing congregational leaders is an important decision. Some groups choose contractors on the basis of the lowest bids submitted. Others choose them on the basis of their size and assets, or on the basis of their reputation for quality workmanship. The question of choosing congregational leaders is a pivotal issue.

Once I was in conversation with a young man exploring ministry in the Mennonite Church. He shared his experience as an assistant minister in another denomination. His congregation was declining because the senior pastor was committing adultery. The tragedy was compounded by the teaching of his denomination which did not allow the congregation to address the problem. To them, leaders are accountable to God alone. The church was to pray and wait for God to discipline and remove him. Meanwhile, the misconduct continued, and no one called him to repentance. While this would not be the practice of most denominations, it represents the extreme of a commonly held attitude toward congregational leadership and authority, that pastors are an elevated elite in the congregation. In this approach to leadership, the congregation is not allowed to choose its contractors.

In some denominations, regional officials appoint the leaders of congregations. In some churches, pastors do not even have their membership in the congregations they serve. Within these denominations, there is a similar *hierarchical* view of authority. Officials in the larger church choose leadership for the local congregation. They would say, "Let the builder choose the contractors."

Still other denominations call their own leaders. In this model, each congregation is free to choose its own leaders. They use trial sermons, search committees, and other kinds of organizational structures to find the right leaders from outside the congregation and bring them in. Much of the discernment is based on the giftedness of the leader and the first impressions made. Usually little is known about their life and walk prior to their candidating. These denominations share a *congregational* view of authority. While quite different from a hierarchical view, it still chooses leadership from outside the congregation. They would say, "Let the buyer choose the contractors."

A small number of denominations are on the other extreme of the leadership and authority question. They do not have designated pastoral leadership. It is neither required nor expected. In these traditions, Christ is seen as the only leader of the church. No person should be in the position reserved for Jesus alone. Positions of responsibility may be rotated so that no one will become a primary leader. In this setting, the goal is for no one to lead except Christ. In reality, there is still leadership, though it is much more subtle and organic. This view is sometimes called *communal* authority. They would say, "Let the buyer be the contractor."

The danger of the hierarchical style is that it can result in domineering and controlling leadership. Communal authority, however, can result in hidden manipulation and stagnation. Historically, churches have tried to find a balance between these two extremes. Jesus specifically said that kingdom authority was not to "lord it over" one another—not even in the guise of being a benefactor (Luke 22:25). But he didn't say there were no gifts of leadership. Instead, he made it clear that each member of the body is valuable (cf. 1 Cor. 12). There is to be no leadership elite, but "the greatest among you must become like the youngest, and the leader like one who serves" (Luke 22:26).

In general, those denominations which emerge from the Roman Catholic tradition tend to be hierarchical. Congregations don't choose their own priests. They are chosen for them. Priests are regarded as being on a higher spiritual plane than others in the congregation. Even among more congregational mainline denominations, pastors are chosen from outside the congregation and brought in to lead. The understanding of Mennonites is congregational when it comes to choosing leadership, but traditionally they tended to choose their leaders from within the congregation. Only in the last century, since they felt the need for specialized training for ministry, have they moved to a more Protestant model.

From the founding moments of the Anabaptist movement, pastors were chosen from the midst of the congregation. If pastors were martyred or imprisoned, new pastors were chosen from within the congregation as soon as possible, "at the same hour," says the Schleitheim Confession of 1527. They were chosen on the basis of the witness and example of their Christian life (Heb. 13:7). Yet they always remained disciples, along with the other members in the local congregation. Pastors, in the Anabaptist-Mennonite tradition, were not some kind of spiritual upper class.

As a result, pastors were given authority on a different basis as well. While most denominations bestow authority based on gifting and after a certain period of education and training, the Anabaptist model placed character ahead of gifting (1 Tim. 3). For Anabaptist-Mennonites, authority was first earned and then conferred. The life of the leader was known before God's call of the leader was recognized. The leader had to be a servant, one who stood by Jesus and his followers in trials (Luke 22:26-28). As this pattern has begun to change, congregations are calling pastors from outside their circle. The result has sometimes been real hurt and misunderstanding as the new pastors try to lead a congregation which is not prepared to follow its leaders until it has first come to know their lives.

 At the same time, congregations have begun to function as though they hired their pastor in the same way an employer hires a worker. But the disciples of Jesus did not hire him to lead them. Instead, they gave him their allegiance and learned from him how to live. Likewise, members can make the task of their pastors a joy or a burden, depending on how they follow (Heb. 13:17). Congregations may give counsel to their pastors, and pastors need to open themselves to dialogue about their ministry. Yet members are also called to submit to their pastors, to be open to be persuaded and led. Congregations are not the management, with pastors simply as employees.

How are we to understand the congregational choosing of leaders? The first church I served as a pastor supplied me with a special gift. It was an understanding of pastoral identity that has given me strength and focus ever since. After being licensed as a pastor for two years, I was being interviewed for ordination. As a requirement for ordination, the conference minister asked the congregation to prepare a written job description for me as pastor.

After several weeks of Bible study, the committee prepared a written statement. While I don't remember much of it, I do remember one sentence: "In salarying a pastor, we are not purchasing a commodity of ministry but are freeing a brother from the need to work additionally to support his family in order that he might be free to give himself to the work of ministry." What they were putting into words was a sense of partnership—a covenant between pastor and congregation (cf. 1 Cor. 9; Gal. 6:6).

The idea of pastoral ministry as a covenant between congregation and leadership was a great gift to a young pastor. There were several parts to that gift. First, they reminded each other that a shepherd's heart cannot be bought. They were not hiring me; they were supporting me. Second, I was a brother, a member with them of the same community of faith.

Finally, ministry was a gift which I was to give back to the congregation. In effect, our covenant was based on mutual submission and trust: They would support my ministry and hold me accountable to God for my walk; I would minister to them and hold them accountable to God for their walk.

Who chooses the contractors? Congregations and pastors choose each other in the presence of God, whose gifts are that some would be leaders (Eph. 4:11).

Seventh Keystone

When the employees of a firm refuse to recognize the authority of the employer to direct their labor, we call it a strike. Sadly, congregations can go on strike by refusing to acknowledge and respect their pastoral leaders. Pastors cannot lead in such a situation, and a congregation cannot continue in such a situation either. To be effective, pastoral authority has to be recognized. If that recognition is withheld, the result is hurt and pain.

At the same time, pastors can try to demand authority to puff up their own ego (Luke 22:24). One who demands authority or attempts to control others operates in another spirit than the Spirit of Jesus. Some congregations have become so wounded by abusive authority that they are reluctant to be led at all. Servant leaders lead by vision and example, not by coercion or control.

This is at the heart of our vision of church. Just as kingdom authority is released to transform lives when we submit ourselves to God's Word rightly understood, so kingdom authority is released to build up communities in love when we submit ourselves to respect and honor servant leaders. So we share the following conviction about the church of Jesus Christ:

We are closer to the vision of Jesus for the church when we see the relationship between congregations and their pastoral leaders as a covenant of mutual trust and submission. Such a relationship is characterized by winsome, supportive, and accountable relationships between congregational members and their pastors.

The church is a community with servant leaders.

This is another characteristic of this vision of church: a congregation released into community through a mutual covenant with servant leaders. To rephrase our motto: Those who know Christ truly, support and respect his servant leaders.

Discussion Questions

1. How have you chosen your most recent pastors? Have they come from outside the congregation or from within?
2. If your congregation has a salaried pastor, do you think of yourselves as hiring or supporting that leader?
3. Are your pastors called on the basis of your knowledge of their life of faith or on the basis of gifting?
4. What could your congregation do to make the ministry of your pastoral leaders more of a joy than a burden?

CHAPTER EIGHT

Getting the Job Done

"Very truly, I tell you, anyone who does not enter the sheepfold by the gate but climbs in by another way is a thief and a bandit. The one who enters by the gate is the shepherd of the sheep. The gatekeeper opens the gate for him, and the sheep hear his voice. He calls his own sheep by name and leads them out. When he has brought out all his own, he goes ahead of them, and the sheep follow him because they know his voice. They will not follow a stranger, but they will run from him because they do not know the voice of strangers."
Jesus used this figure of speech with them, but they did not understand what he was saying to them. So again Jesus said to them, "Very truly, I tell you, I am the gate for the sheep. All who came before me are thieves and bandits; but the sheep did not listen to them. I am the gate. Whoever enters by me will be saved, and will come in and go out and find pasture. The thief comes only to steal and kill and destroy. I came that they may have life, and have it abundantly. (John 10:1-10)

Good Builders
Trait No. 1: They Care About What They Are Building

Keep watch over yourselves and over all the flock, of which the Holy Spirit has made you overseers, to shepherd the church of God that he obtained with the blood of his own Son. I know that after I have gone, savage wolves will come in among you, not sparing the flock. (Acts 20:28-29)

Trait No. 2: They Don't Just Collect a Paycheck

I exhort the elders among you to tend the flock of God that is in your charge, exercising the oversight, not under compulsion but willingly, as God would have you do it—not for sordid gain but eagerly. Do not lord it over those in your charge, but be examples to the flock. And when the chief shepherd appears, you will win the crown of glory that never fades away. (1 Pet. 5:1c-4)

Trait No. 3: They Are Conscientious

In the presence of God and of Christ Jesus, who is to judge the living and the dead, and in view of his appearing and his kingdom, I solemnly urge you: proclaim the message; be persistent whether the time is favorable or unfavorable; convince, rebuke, and encourage, with the utmost patience in teaching. . . . As for you, always be sober, endure suffering, do the work of an evangelist, carry out your ministry fully.

(2 Tim. 4:1-2, 5)

Getting Down to Work

Several years ago the middle school our children attended was enlarged. The blueprints were approved, the bond issue was passed, and the contractor hired. But the construction was repeatedly delayed because of all kinds of problems. The contractor missed almost every deadline. The main reason was that he also was building another structure at the same time and didn't have enough workers. The other contract had a penalty clause in it. To avoid paying fines on that building, he put most of his workers on the other building and hired untested workers for the middle school. They were simply not getting the job done on schedule.

When Jesus builds his church, he will see to it that the job gets done (Matt. 16:18). He chooses leaders who will build according to his plan. We have already seen how kingdom authority is released in personal transformation when we obey the Word of God. We have seen how kingdom authority is released to build community in love when there is a mutual covenant between leaders and congregation. But using the correct blueprints and choosing the right contractors still leaves us at the beginning of the task. What about authority to build?

Not just anyone can go onto a construction site and begin to build a building. The workers need to be skilled at what they are doing. Masons, carpenters, plumbers, electricians—all contribute to the project. In the same way certain gifts are needed to build up a faith community from the raw materials of individual believers. Not just anyone can go onto the spiritual construction site and build a faith community. Then who does have the authority and responsibility to do it? By now the answer is clear: pastoral leaders.

In the Roman Catholic tradition, priests have a unique role in the congregation because only the priests are given authority to perform the sacraments. The sacrament of the mass is central to being church in that tradition, and the priest administers that rite. In the Protestant tradition, pastors have a unique office because only they are sufficiently trained to preach and teach biblical doctrine. The preaching of the Word is central to being church in that tradition, and only the pastors can really do it.

But neither administration of the sacrament nor carrying out the office of preacher-teacher transforms a collection of individual believers into a faith community. In the

Anabaptist-Mennonite tradition, the primary task of pastoral leadership is to assemble individual believers into a community of faith. The members discern the will of the Spirit and give their pastors authority for that people-making purpose (Acts 15:28; 20:28). While pastors may baptize, preach, and officiate at communion, they do this in order to accomplish their primary task, which is to shape and develop this alternative faith community. This is a fundamentally different understanding both of authority and ministry.

Jesus said the True Shepherd was different from the stranger because he knew his sheep by name. The sheep would follow their shepherd because they recognized his voice. In other words, pastors have authority to lead based on their personal relationship with the members of the congregation and with the Chief Shepherd, Jesus Christ (1 Pet. 5:4). To function as a pastor according to Jesus' vision requires developing personal relationships. Such authority is earned and then conferred.

Jesus said the Gate Shepherd was different from the thief and the robber because he cares for the sheepfold. At the time of Jesus, many shepherds would bring their flocks home at night and return them to the sheepfold. Several flocks of sheep would share the sheepfold, and each shepherd would take turns sleeping at the gate. Such a shepherd was called "The Gate." This is the image Jesus is using. By doing so, he is saying that his pastoral leaders watch over the boundaries of the faith community. They are to see that true believers don't wander out and that pretenders don't get in. Pastoral leaders gain the trust of their congregation by caring for the boundaries of the faith community.

Jesus also said the Good Shepherd was different from the hired hand because he cared for the flock. He did not run when the wolf came. He remained faithful in the time of crisis. Pastors gain the loyalty of their members by their faithful care in times of crisis. Authority based on relationships, trust based on watchfulness, and loyalty based on faithfulness are marks of Jesus' builders. They get the job done.

But precisely because pastors have authority, they also can abuse it. It is naive for the church to assume that if they get the right kind of spiritual leaders, there will be no more problems with abusive authority. While we may institute safeguards, we must recognize how "power tends to corrupt" its owners (Lord Acton). Congregations must understand that even the most godly leaders face the seductive effects of power and authority. That is one major reason to pray for those in authority.

Anabaptist-Mennonite churches traditionally had a ministry team (Acts 14:23). They were convinced that a group of pastoral leaders can bring a balance and an ability to recognize and avoid abuse much better than a single pastor. Because the potential for abuse or distortion is greater if the pastoral leader stands alone, teams provide safety.

The New Testament model repeatedly is that of ministry teams. Often these pastoral leaders are called elders in the New Testament. Their authority is a collective authority rather than being based on individual power. They recognize that they have authority to lead in light of their unity with each other as a team and in faithfulness to God. Kingdom authority to build the faith community is released as pastors minister in unity as a team.

Such pastoral teams model the kind of mutual submission that releases the love of God in the faith community. The leaders can model healthy ways of dealing with differences. Many people live with the fear of conflict and try to avoid it by papering over differences. The results are usually greater hurt and misunderstanding down the road. As elders work through differences, they demonstrate how the whole congregation can continue to maintain unity even amid disagreement.

Eighth Keystone

Authority earned from relationships, trust from watchfulness, loyalty from faithfulness, and confidence from a healthy unity—these are characteristics of the kinds of workers Jesus uses to build his church. Congregations can withhold cooperation and hinder God's plan. Pastoral leaders can abuse their authority and distort God's purposes. But we still share a fundamental conviction about the nature of the church of Jesus Christ:

> We are closer to the vision of Jesus for the church when we see pastoral authority given leaders so they can build individual believers into a faith community. Such authority is earned through personal relationships of watchfulness and faithfulness. It is collective authority exercised out of the unity of a ministry team.
> *The church is a community of servant leaders.*

This completes another characteristic of our vision of church. Jesus' church is a people of mutual submission who are released into community through relationships of love and trust with their pastoral leaders.

Discussion Questions

1. Put into your own words the difference between Roman Catholic, Protestant, and Anabaptist views of pastoral ministry.
2. With what understanding of pastoral ministry did you grow up? What is the current understanding in your congregation?

3. Do you have personal memories of pastoral leaders who have abused their authority? What effect did it have on the congregation? On you?
4. What could your congregation do to strengthen its ministry team, if you have one? If you don't, what could your congregation do to develop one?

A Practice of Spirituality

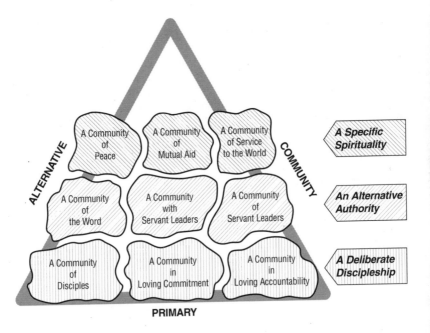

CHAPTER NINE

The Wrecking Ball

Indeed, we live as human beings, but we do not wage war according to human standards; for the weapons of our warfare are not merely human, but they have divine power to destroy strongholds. We destroy arguments and every proud obstacle raised up against the knowledge of God, and we take every thought captive to obey Christ. We are ready to punish every disobedience when your obedience is complete.

(2 Cor. 10:3-6)

Three Arguments for Preservation

Witness No. 1: An Unnamed Witness, 1529

But the law and the sword of this world sever a man from his life in body and soul, even though he should desire to amend his life immediately. . . . Therefore, if Christ is really to count for something here in his kingdom, which is not material but spiritual, . . . the servant must give way, with his literalistic law, for a spiritual kingdom cannot carry nor use a material sword. . . . Our king Christ is a spiritual king and has an eternal kingdom, wherefore his sword dare not be material but spiritual.

Witness No. 2: Peter Riedemann
Important Hutterite Leader, 1542

Christ has not come to destroy men—therefore his disciples also refuse to do so; for he says, "Know ye not of what Spirit ye are the children?" as though he would say, "Doth the Spirit of grace teach you to destroy, or will ye walk according to the flesh and forsake the Spirit, whose children ye have become?"[19]

Witness No. 3: Menno Simons
Dutch Anabaptist Writer, 1552

The Scriptures teach that there are two opposing princes and two opposing kingdoms: the one is the Prince of peace, the other the prince of strife. Each of these princes has his particular kingdom, and as the prince is, so is also the kingdom. The Prince of peace is Christ Jesus; his kingdom is the kingdom of peace, which is his church. . . . True Christians do not know vengeance, no matter how they are mistreated.[20]

Bring in the Wrecking Ball?

Recently I heard a prominent pastor on the radio. He began to preach about Jesus' teaching on forgiveness and nonviolence. Carefully he reviewed what Jesus said about loving enemies, turning the other cheek, and not repaying evil for evil. He agreed that taking life was forbidden by Christ. He said Jesus taught the way of forgiving love in the face of conflict and violence. I was ready for him to conclude that warfare is wrong for Christians. But just when he could have reached a simple conclusion about the way of Christ, he said, "But when we come to warfare to defend our country, we must be practical."

I felt like someone had brought in the wrecking ball. All of the teachings of Jesus—truths he had affirmed—were smashed to the ground with the simple statement, "We must be practical." It floored me to hear him say it.

But the more I reflected, the more I realized how typical it was of the reactions of our contemporary society to the reality of violence. Even the Christian "establishment" has concluded that a nonviolent response to violence is not "practical," but that a violent response is.

We could spend a long time discussing whether warfare is really "practical." But the point here is that the church of Jesus cannot be signed over to the prevailing view of society based on what is supposedly practical. The result is like erecting a building, only to have someone else come in and smash it to the ground. Our society is ready to tolerate Christians who let their faith be divided into what is spiritual and what is "practical." They will be glad to let the spiritual be shaped by Jesus' life and teaching, so long as *the world can determine what is practical.*

This separation of personal piety and lifestyle is disastrous to the community of faith. It allows believers to be distinctive in their witness to personal beliefs regarding sexuality, abortion, pornography, etc. But when it comes to living the lifestyle of Jesus, Christian beliefs must be subordinate to the views of society, which has concluded that violence is the only practical response to violence. Therefore, no matter what Jesus teaches, we must be practical. We have to use our guns to put down the enemy.

However, Jesus taught us to love our enemies (personal and national) and pray for those who persecute us (Matt. 5:44). He taught us not to resist an evil person but to turn the other cheek (Matt. 5:39). He rebuked his disciple Peter for trying to defend him with a sword, saying that violent means only lead to violent ends (Matt. 26:52). When ·he was interrogated before Pilate, he affirmed that his kingdom was "not from this world," like other kingdoms. His servants would not resort to life-threatening force, even to prevent his arrest (John 18:36). Our value system must come from the life and teachings of Jesus.

Several years ago I was walking onto a subway platform in London, England, to catch a train home from
downtown. As I turned the corner from the hallway to the
platform, a rough and imposing man slammed up against
me and grabbed me by the shirt collar. He lifted me off the
ground and pushed me back into a hallway. The stranger
was angry and abusive and mumbled something to me
that I did not fully understand.

Suddenly I was confronted face-to-face with violence.
The way I responded was not the result of a carefully
thought-out ethic of nonviolence. My response was not
fear or anger but puzzlement. I looked at the man and
asked, "What's the matter here?" He stopped in his tracks
and stared at me, obviously confused.

All of a sudden, I sensed something profound had happened. The anger in his spirit did not meet any anger in
mine. The results were disarming. There was nothing
there to continue to fuel his anger. He let go of me and
walked off, mumbling to himself. I walked away un-
harmed. I guessed that the man was taking some kind of
drug. He did not seem to be open to reason. Nonetheless,
the result was a peaceful resolution of the conflict. Who
said nonviolence is not practical?

After the incident, I was a little shaky for a while. Then
I began reflecting on the experience. I wondered what
would have happened to me if I had just watched a *Rambo*
movie or had been filling my spirit with the rhetoric and
fears of our age. My first reaction would likely have been
much different. I certainly would have been more angry. I
might even have been violent, and the outcome would certainly have been different. Jesus was right. What you have
in your heart comes out in your actions—especially in
times of crisis.

Contemporary ethicist Ron Sider asked the question
this way: "Why is it that when soldiers die while killing

others, we call them heroes, but when Christians die because they refuse to kill, we call them fools?"[21] That statement well describes the position of the kind of Christianity our society promotes: There is no basic conflict between national patriotism and the kingdom of God, only between the "lofty" teachings of Jesus and the "practical" solutions to life.

If we are going to build the community of faith according to the vision of Jesus, we cannot consign it to the values of society. We must use the gospel crane for lifting the rafters into place rather than swinging a wrecking ball to punish evil persons or nations. Instead of separating spirituality into two spheres, we must keep them together. Jesus calls us to rely on the presence and power of the Holy Spirit, not just to produce an inner piety. We are to pray for those who persecute us and also to produce an outward holiness, to be peacemakers, to help enemies become friends of God and of each other (Matt. 5:9; 2 Cor. 5:18). Thus we rely on God to deliver us or to settle matters in his own way and time. We refuse to compromise the teaching and example of Jesus in the face of "practical necessities" of human violence. We can respond to violence with love, even if it might mean suffering (Matt. 5:10-12, 44-48; Rom. 12:14-21).

In effect, we are renouncing the power of this world (violence and warfare) for the power of God's kingdom. The Holy Spirit enables us to proclaim a response to violence other than life-threatening force. We recognize there is a basic conflict between national superpatriotism and giving highest allegiance to the kingdom of God. Martyrs, not soldiers, become our heroes. We declare that God's reign commands ultimate allegiance and authority. We hold to an uncompromising commitment to follow Christ in life, a commitment to the way of peace through radical reliance on the Holy Spirit.

Mennonite practice has included conscientious opposition to military service and to holding public office where conscience might be compromised. Many Mennonites maintained the doctrine of nonresistance in the face of wartime fervor, even when it brought persecution or mass migration. Central to Mennonite identity is the affirmation that a community of faith must live by a radically different spirit than the violence of this world. Mennonite believers have continued to confess the way of love in the midst of suffering.

In some current settings, this affirmation of faith may have become separated from its spiritual roots and appear to be simply a legalistic dogma or a humanistic ethic. As a result, the practice of nonresistance has been reduced to being "against war." In addition, cooperation with others who pursue peace (for completely different reasons) may have given the appearance that there is no distinction between Christian nonviolence and humanistic or new-age pacifism. But the vision of church which we affirm is a Christ-centered commitment to nonretaliation, making peace, and responding with love.

The true community of faith is a people of peace, empowered by the Spirit to "pursue peace with everyone" (Heb. 12:14). They choose to respond to violence with love, not simply because it is a correct understanding of Scripture, although it is that. Nor is it simply because Jesus commanded it, although he did. Ultimately, the commitment to nonresistance is a personal response to Jesus; it cannot be legislated. It is the way of the faith community because it is part of the very character of Jesus Christ himself. The Spirit of Jesus, who is grieved by bitterness and rage and anger and cursing (Eph. 4:30-31), cannot bless the taking of human life for any reason.

Ninth Keystone

The way for disciples of Jesus is to respond to violence with suffering love. This uncompromising commitment to the way of peace is a part of the very spirituality of the faith community and its confession of Jesus. It leads to times of serious intercessory prayer, with the faith community relying on the power of the Holy Spirit. Members resist the way of violence, which is a quest for power and control over others. So we share the following conviction about the nature of the church of Jesus Christ:

> We are closer to the vision of Jesus Christ for the church when we choose not to compromise the Spirit of Jesus with the violence of the world in which we live. Suffering love rather than life-threatening force is the way of Jesus in response to violence.
> *The church is a community of peace.*

Peter Riedemann, an early Hutterite, wrote: " 'To them of old it is said, "An eye for an eye and a tooth for a tooth," but I say unto you, that you resist not evil!' Here Christ makes a distinction himself. There is no need for many words, for it is clear that Christians can neither go to war nor practice vengeance. Whosoever does this has forsaken and denied Christ and Christ's nature."[22]

In this simple statement, Riedemann summarizes a characteristic of church which Mennonites hold dear. The church is an alternative community, partly because of the different spirit it affirms. The Spirit of Jesus affirms the character of Jesus. We cannot afford to let the wrecking ball of society's values change the character of the church. Our confession is based on Jesus Christ and his way of peacemaking.

Discussion Questions

1. When you were growing up, what position did your group take on warfare and nonviolence? Is it different from the stance of your congregation today?

2. Is there a difference between an "ethic" of nonviolence and a "spirituality" of nonviolence? How would you describe that difference?

3. What could your congregation do to cultivate its spiritual life of nonviolence and nonretaliation?

4. Is there a clear sense in your congregation that the value system of the believer is different from the value system of society?

CHAPTER TEN

Paying the Bills

After he had washed their feet, had put on his robe, and had returned to the table, he said to them, "Do you know what I have done to you? You call me Teacher and Lord—and you are right, for that is what I am. So if I, your Lord and Teacher, have washed your feet, you also ought to wash one another's feet. For I have set you an example, that you also should do as I have done to you. Very truly, I tell you, servants are not greater than their master, nor are messengers greater than the one who sent them. If you know these things, you are blessed if you do them. (John 13:12-17)

Three Benefactors

Benefactor No. 1: The First Church at Pentecost

There was not a needy person among them, for as many as owned lands or houses sold them and brought the proceeds of what was sold. They laid it at the apostles' feet, and it was distributed to each as any had need. (Acts 4:34-35)

Benefactor No. 2: A Woman Named Tabitha

Now in Joppa there was a disciple whose name was Tabitha,

which in Greek is Dorcas. She was devoted to good works and acts of charity. . . . So Peter got up and went with them; and when he arrived, they took him to the room upstairs. All the widows stood beside him, weeping and showing tunics and other clothing that Dorcas had made while she was with them. (Acts 9:36, 39)

Benefactor No. 3: The Macedonian Christians

We want you to know, brothers and sisters, about the grace of God that has been granted to the churches of Macedonia; for during a severe ordeal of affliction, their abundant joy and their extreme poverty have overflowed in a wealth of generosity on their part. For, as I can testify, they voluntarily gave according to their means, and even beyond their means. (2 Cor. 8:1-3)

Picking up the Pieces

Once I read of a construction company that had won the bid on a major construction project. In the middle of the construction, however, one of the subcontractors defaulted. Suddenly the whole project was in turmoil. Materials had been ordered but not paid for. Workers had been hired and demanded their wages. The construction company had to assume responsibility for the subcontractor and was facing bankruptcy as a result.

I remembered our first experiences with the Mennonite Church. There we were, I with two years of postgraduate studies completed, and Sue pregnant with our first child. I had quit my studies to begin serving as a pastor of a small Mennonite congregation. Suddenly we discovered that the non-Mennonite medical insurance we had carefully kept current was being terminated before the child's birth. We were faced with major medical bills and no insurance. Our next trip to the physician was difficult. We had to explain to him that we would not have the money to pay his fees immediately. He seemed understanding.

The following visit was no easier—until we met with our physician, who welcomed us with good news. On his own, he had spoken to the area Mennonite congregations and asked for their help. When all was said and done, our entire medical bill was paid. We were dumbstruck. This was "mutual aid," we were told. It was the way Christians cared for one another.

In the years that followed, we had more than one occasion to witness the same phenomenon. A young family whose baby eventually died of cancer received help for uncovered expenses not only from area congregations but also from Mennonite Mutual Aid—even though they had medical insurance with another company through the husband's work.

We established a mutual-aid fund in our congregation, composed of 10 percent of our offerings (cf. Acts 6:1-6). It went to pay for orthodontic work for a single mother, deposits for rental apartments, and even paid the debts of members of the church who were between jobs and going under financially. Although never a written pledge, we had a commitment to one another not to let anyone in our congregation go without food, shelter, or clothing.

Since most of our members were from other church backgrounds or had no previous church experience, we worked out our own way of caring for one another based on our early experiences. It was encouraging to discover similar practices in other Mennonite congregations. This was ministry to one another within the community of faith. It was our understanding of "being church" together.

Yes, we struggled not to develop a "welfare mentality." When people came to us in need as a result of their disobedience to God, we had to deal with our own attitudes. We did more than our share of financial counseling. But we learned something about love and grace in the process. More and more we realized that for the most part, the world is not made up of people who have grown up in strong, loving homes with good principles of money management instilled in them. They needed our love and guidance, not our judgment. To see families come through to strength was what kept us going.

Not till several years later did I begin to reflect on the radically different nature of church which this kind of behavior represents. In most congregations, the offerings are for the pastor's salary, the building, and the programs. That the congregation should feel some responsibility for one another as members is unusual. Individual acts of charity do happen in most of them. But the understanding that it is the responsibility of the congregation to care for one another is not common.

I recently attended a meeting of pastors where we began to discuss this issue to test my own perceptions. I said that within the Anabaptist circle of churches, if someone in our congregations lost a house or went bankrupt and the congregation didn't help, we would feel that something had broken down in the life of the congregation. One pastor who had grown up in another setting was taken aback. He could not believe this was a shared understanding of church. This pastor was overwhelmed and excited. He resolved to go back to his congregation and begin calling forth the same kind of caring.

Fundamentally, the issue is whether, in the church, believers are responsible for each other (Gal. 6:2) or simply responsible for themselves. Do we care for each other in need, or is the government responsible for the "less fortunate"? Worse yet, do we assume that Christians will never have those kinds of needs if they just trust God and obey him? If our style of Christianity is only to preach the Word and evangelize the lost, we have severely limited the nature of the church. We are in danger of defaulting on our contract and leaving the bills unpaid.

The practice of our Anabaptist-Mennonite tradition is much different. From the radical witness of the Hutterites, who shared all things in common, to the Swiss-German Brethren, who helped to care for each other's needs, the principle of mutual aid has been embedded in our history. In the twentieth century, we practice sharing labor in harvesting crops, in barn-raising, in helping those struck by disaster, and in doing work and bringing in food for the sick neighbor. All these show how we apply the principle of mutual aid.

Jesus modeled this ministry of service as he washed his disciples' feet. This most demeaning of tasks was performed by the host of the meal. When he finished, he called his disciples to do the same (John 13:14). Jesus said serving one another brought a joy and a peace which the love of position and possessions could never give (Luke 12:15). He told his followers that it was more blessed to give than to receive (Acts 20:35). Our Master said that if we understood these things, we would be blessed if we did them (John 13:17). Ministry to the poor and needy would be ministry to the King himself (Matt. 25:40).

Tenth Keystone

This is another characteristic of our vision of church: loving ministry to those in need. Congregations who live out this understanding of church are characterized by humility. Concern for the needs of others is not understood as "charity" but as doing justice, loving kindness, and walking humbly with our God (Mic. 6:8). While welfare systems and charity tend to be impersonal, mutual aid is personal. Ministry to those in need comes out of a recognition that someday we or our children could be in the same situation.

Ulrich Stadler, an early Anabaptist, wrote the following: "In brief, a brother should serve, live, and work for the other, none for himself; indeed, one household for another, one community for another, . . . wherever the Lord grants it that we gather together, one communion, as a body of the Lord and members one to another. . . . Such is the life of the elect, holy children of God in their pilgrimage."[23] Therefore, we share the following conviction about the nature of the church of Jesus Christ:

> We are closer to the vision of Christ for the church when, in humility, we care for the needs of one another within the faith community.
> *The church is a community of mutual aid.*

A congregation rooted in a commitment to follow Christ together as brothers and sisters, a congregation in a supportive partnership with its pastoral leaders. Such a congregation will care for the needs of one another. In their love for each another, they will respond in such a way that there will be no needy among them. Is that what characterizes your congregation?

Discussion Questions

1. What has been your experience of mutual aid in your church upbringing?
2. Should believers in a congregation have a mutual commitment to provide food, shelter, and clothing for one another in time of need?
3. What method do you have in your own congregation to address mutual-aid needs? If you don't have one, should you? What would it look like?
4. What could your congregation do to nourish its life and witness of mutual care?

CHAPTER ELEVEN

Temples or Tents?

Do not store up for yourselves treasures on earth, where moth and rust consume and where thieves break in and steal; but store up for yourselves treasures in heaven, where neither moth nor rust consumes and where thieves do not break in and steal. For where your treasure is, there your heart will be also. . . .

No one can serve two masters; for a slave will either hate the one and love the other, or be devoted to the one and despise the other. You cannot serve God and wealth.

(Matt. 6:19-21, 24)

Three Testimonies
Testimony No. 1: Balthasar Hubmaier
Early Anabaptist Scholar, 1526

Always and everywhere I have said as follows, . . . that each [one] should have regard for [the] neighbor, so that the hungry might be fed, the thirsty refreshed, the naked clothed. For we are not lords of our own property, but stewards and dispensers. . . . Rather we would say: if anyone would take your cloak, give him your coat also.[24]

93

Testimony No. 2: Dirk Philips
Dutch Anabaptist Leader, 1558

Thus the rich, who have received many temporal possessions from the Lord, are to minister to the poor therewith (Rom. 15:27; 2 Cor. 8:10) and supply their need, so that the poor in turn serve them as they may have need of their services.[25]

Testimony No. 3: Menno Simons
Dutch Anabaptist Writer, about 1539

True evangelical faith is of such a nature that it cannot lie dormant, but manifests itself in all righteousness and works of love; it dies unto the flesh and blood; . . . it seeks and serves and fears God; it clothes the naked; it feeds the hungry; it comforts the sorrowful; it shelters the destitute; it aids and consoles the sad; it returns good for evil; it serves those that harm it; it prays for those that persecute it; . . . it seeks that which is lost; it binds up that which is wounded; it heals that which is diseased, and it saves that which is sound; it has become all things to all [people].[26]

Tent Cities

After a recent hurricane struck the southern United States, the government responded to the massive loss of homes by erecting tent cities. This was a simple and efficient way to respond to the crisis because it provided shelter quickly and at low cost. Imagine the reaction if, instead, government officials had started to build permanent shelters—construction that could have taken many months while people remained homeless. The world would have been outraged at such a ridiculous, self-defeating response.

However, a certain cycle can develop in congregations, and over time, it is equally self-defeating. When the mission of the church becomes focused on the *programs* of the

church, and the purpose of the church is reduced to recruiting workers to run the programs to help recruit workers to run the programs, etc., then the church begins to become unresponsive to the needs around it. The vision of
such a church has stopped being that of Jesus: Go and
preach the gospel (Mark 16:15). Instead, it seems to say,
"Come, attend our program."

These congregations erect temples rather than tents.
They seem more concerned with building monuments to
God than touching people's lives. This is not the vision of
Jesus. The compassion of Christ motivates the church to
reach out to those who are in need. That was central to the
earthly ministry of Jesus. In the parable of the good Samar-
itan, Jesus taught that loving one's neighbor also includes
those outside the faith community (Luke 10:25-37). Jesus
used the parable of the sheep and the goats to show how
the loving response to the hungry, naked, sick, and imprisoned is really a response to him (Matt. 25:31-46).

The simple truth is that, no matter how loving a church
is to its own members, if it exists only for itself, it dies. Real
fulfillment comes partly from reaching out to the needs of
others. This requires a different understanding of church.
John 3:16 does not say, "God so loved the church"; it says,
"God so loved the world." Being filled with the Spirit of Jesus includes understanding that the heart of God is for the
hurting people of this world. Just as the Spirit of Jesus
compels us to confront violence with love, it compels us to
care for the hurting. We cannot sit idly by, ignore the sick
and suffering, and continue with our "holy huddles."

True compassion within the faith community—genuine mutual aid—quickly extends itself to others. This has
been the experience of the Anabaptist-Mennonite churches. In response to the deep need of Russian Mennonites after World War I, Mennonite Central Committee was established in 1920 to provide relief for hungry and suffering

Mennonite sisters and brothers. Since its beginnings, MCC has enlarged its vision so that the agency now helps the hungry and suffering all around the world. Its motto, "In the Name of Christ" sums up the motivation that even draws individuals from other denominations and faith traditions to volunteer their services.

Mennonite Disaster Service emerged in the years that followed and responded to natural disasters in North America. Through its ministries, victims of hurricanes (like those in Florida and Louisiana), floods, storms, and tornadoes have experienced the care of Mennonite Christians. Such service ministries have shown the unique character of Mennonites.

Some have talked about this trait of church as a "spirituality of service." There is truth in that description. The emphasis of Reformation spirituality was on grace through faith. This had a tendency to undervalue the role of good works. What was truly important was reduced to "believing" and "receiving." The Anabaptist movement also resonated with James when he said that faith without works is dead (James 2:17). What is truly important is not just believing and receiving the things of faith, but living them as well. Good deeds are a natural part of biblical faith.

This spirituality of service has helped to reinforce the biblical understanding of nonviolence. In many global situations, warfare has fed poverty and human suffering. When we are involved in ministering to the suffering and in proclaiming the way of nonviolence, this gives integrity to the witness of the church. The goal of both is to live by the Spirit of Jesus.

Such involvement in the needs of the world also helps the church face the issues of wealth and poverty. In Luke, Jesus gave us a number of warnings about the dangers of wealth. He concluded that riches can choke out the life of God (Luke 8:14). He said that material things can make a person anxious and insecure (12:22-24). Riches can blind us from seeing eternal values (16:19-23). They can begin to control us (16:13). And riches can even blind us to the eternal consequences of our actions (12:19-20). Finally, wealth can actually be a curse if it keeps us from surrendering to Jesus Christ (Matt. 19:16-26).

Fundamentally, the church does not just exist for itself and its own needs. The church exists for the sake of the world. Ministry is not limited to the preaching of the gospel and the teaching of the Word. Ministry is the work of the whole church as it reaches out to the needs of the world. Too often the contemporary church has built temples and confined its ministry to what could happen within those four walls. We must learn again how to build tents.

Eleventh Keystone

Expanding this characteristic of the vision, we can say that the church of Jesus Christ is a community with compassion for the suffering people of the world. While we have a primary responsibility for those in need within the faith community, the church does not exist simply for itself. It exists for the world.

Part of the response to this need and to Jesus' teachings on wealth and prosperity is to live more simply and to give generously. A simple lifestyle is a Christian response to the hungry and suffering of our world. The church does exist for those beyond its doors. We share the following conviction about the nature of the church of Jesus Christ:

> We are closer to the vision of Christ for the church when, in compassion, we care for the suffering and needy in the world as well as the needs of one another within the faith community.
> *The church is a community service to the world.*

A congregation which begins in a commitment to follow Christ together as brothers and sisters, a congregation which supports and partners with its pastoral leaders— members of such a congregation will begin to care for the needs of one another. In their love for each other, they will respond in such a way that there will be no needy among them. As a response to God's compassion for the world, they will share what they have with those who are in need, even beyond their membership. Such is the Spirit of Jesus in the church.

Discussion Questions

1. How would you describe your congregation? Is it more like a tent or a temple?
2. What has been your experience of doing ministry to needy people? What impact did it have on your faith in Christ? On theirs?
3. Do people in your community see your congregation as a faith community that truly cares for their needs? Or is your congregation isolated from many of the real needs in your neighborhood?
4. What could your congregation do to undergird its ministry to the needs of the community in which it is primarily working?

A Life of
Invitation

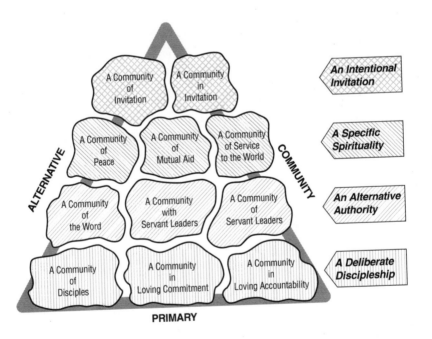

CHAPTER TWELVE

No More Museums

You are the salt of the earth; but if salt has lost its taste, how can its saltiness be restored? It is no longer good for anything, but is thrown out and trampled under foot.

You are the light of the world. A city built on a hill cannot be hid. No one after lighting a lamp puts it under the bushel basket, but on the lampstand, and it gives light to all in the house. In the same way, let your light shine before others, so that they may see your good works and give glory to your Father in heaven. (Matt. 5:13-16)

The Witness of Menno Simons

Display No. 1: A Passionate Message

We desire with ardent hearts even at the cost of life and blood that the holy gospel of Jesus Christ and his apostles, . . . may be taught and preached through all the world as the Lord Jesus Christ commanded his disciples as a last word to them while he was on earth (Matt. 28:19; Mark 16:15).[27]

Display No. 2: A Fresh Perspective

We seek, teach, and desire a true faith and Christian life conformable to the doctrine of Jesus Christ and his apostles, for the doctrine of the preachers is all vain and useless if the Word which is preached is not accepted by faith; . . . and faith is vain and dead before God when it does not work by love (Heb. 4:2; James 2:20).[28]

Display No. 3: An Earnest Appeal

If you sincerely accepted and believed the divine goodness, mercy, and the boundless love of our beloved Lord Jesus Christ toward you, namely, that, by his burning love, he became a humble mortal man for you; came down from high heaven into these lower parts of the earth; in love taught and preached unto you the eternal kingdom of God; in love performed miracles, in love prayed, suffered tribulation, anxiety, arrest in prison; in love was beaten, mocked, derided, spit upon, scourged, crowned with thorns, drank gall and vinegar, was blasphemed, crucified, dead, and buried for you; in love was raised up, has ascended to heaven, is seated at the right hand of the Father, and by his crimson blood became your faithful servant, Intercessor, Atoner, Savior, Mediator, and Advocate; if you believe that by love he sent to you and to the whole world his faithful servants, his holy apostles, with the Word of grace—if you believed all this, you would doubtlessly love him in return, him who has shown you such great love and grace without any merit on your part. And if you would return the love with which he has loved you and yet loves you, you would, believe me, not tire of seeking and following him, so that you might live unblamably according to his blessed will, and walk all your life in his divine commandments.[29]

Exhibit or Living Demonstration?

I was amused the first time I heard a tongue-in-cheek definition of the church: "The Society for the Preservation of the Memory of Jesus Christ." Then I was amazed as the meaning began to soak in. Finally, I became sad. I realized that this definition of church is often more accurate than we care to admit, especially for those who are on the out-side looking in. The church can feel a bit like a museum dedicated to preserving old-fashioned ideas and traditions about God and religion.

It may also be more accurate than we care to admit for many who are actively a part of a traditional congregation. Even though we know the real meaning of Easter and un-derstand that Jesus was raised from the dead, nonetheless we can live from Sunday to Sunday carrying on with the program as though Jesus is not alive and active today. As one person told me, "If Jesus really wanted to say some-thing in my congregation, he'd either have to tell the preacher three weeks in advance or try awfully hard to get a word in during the announcements." However, Jesus didn't come to build museums!

Once a woman whose church experience included en-thusiastic worship decided to tour Europe for a vacation. One Sunday morning she found herself in England visit-ing an Anglican cathedral. During the sermon she enthusi-astically shouted, "Amen, brother!" This brought an usher to her pew with a polite inquiry. She explained her behav-ior, "I have Jesus in my heart." The usher replied, "What-ever it is you've got, you didn't get it here."

Jesus said the faith community was a city set on a hill and a light on a stand. The church is to be a visible commu-nity, not something hidden. It is to be visible for a purpose. But what are we to be visible for? Are we a museum to the life and memory of Jesus Christ? Or are we a living dem-onstration? Jesus wants his church to be a living, breathing example of his life and ministry on the earth.

The point of being visible is to cause others to glorify God. In other words, the church should live in such a way that people recognize the Lord behind their life and ac-tions. *The church is a community in witness.* Every faith com-munity has a history and tradition. If that history and tradition serve us well, they point beyond themselves to the Lord of all history. But if we stop with tradition, the church at that point becomes a museum, not a faith community. We wonder about faith: Will they get it here? Will people recognize in our life together the presence of Jesus? Are we a museum to the memory of Jesus, or a faith community which is alive with the presence of God?

The congregation built on a genuine commitment to love one another as Jesus loved us will cooperate with servant leaders and strive to become a community of love. Members of such a community will be actively involved in meeting the needs of one another and the needs of others outside the faith community. This witness of love and compassion points to the one who with love and compassion laid down his life for others. The invitation can be: "Let anyone who is thirsty come to [Jesus]" (John 7:37).

The congregation built on a clear commitment to follow Christ in life will obey his teaching and example as revealed in the Bible. The congregation obedient to the Scriptures will respond to the violence of this world as Jesus did, in the Spirit of love, without retaliating. Their witness of suffering love points to the one who suffered in love for a lost world. This witness has integrity. We invite others, "Be imitators of me, as I am of Christ" (1 Cor. 11:1).

Our invitation is for everyone to know Christ Jesus and to follow him. Jesus said, "Come to me, all you that are weary and are carrying heavy burdens, and I will give you rest. Take my yoke upon you, and learn from me; for I am gentle and humble in heart, and you will find rest for your souls. For my yoke is easy, and my burden is light" (Matt. 11:28-30). When we invite others to come to Jesus, we welcome them with his love and grace. We follow Jesus as we take his yoke upon ourselves. The rest for our souls comes in knowing and following our Master.

Jesus calls the church beyond "personal evangelism."

Jesus' way, in effect, is *corporate* evangelism. Evangelism is not just something each person does in isolation from fellow believers. Instead, it is the witness of the entire community of faith. There is something of the life of Jesus in our life together that we want others to experience! Our life together in Jesus is our best gospel tract. But a witness of deeds is not complete without a witness of words.

An elder in a congregation in which I was a pastor had as his motto, "Live your life in such a way that people will want to know Christ." One day he came late to the coffee break at work. He overheard two men talking about him. One said, "That Jonas is certainly a fine man." The other responded, "Yes, I could never be like him." Suddenly Jonas realized that the goodness of his life was not enough to point others to the Savior. They gave him the honor for his moral life and concluded that they could never be good enough. He realized that they needed to know the "why" of his life, not just the "what."

The task of evangelism is really a two-sided endeavor. First, it is a witness of lifestyle. We must be able to point with integrity to our faith community in the confidence that "here is an example of what we mean when we talk about knowing and following Jesus." We are not perfect, but with God's help, we are trying to live in the way of Jesus. Second, it is a witness of words. We must be able to swing open the faith community's doors of love and say: "We want you to come, to know and follow Jesus with us."

Twelfth Keystone

This is another mark of the Mennonite vision: the church is a faith community actively inviting others to the same life of faith. We are a people of invitation, compelled by the Spirit of Jesus to welcome all through a new birth into a life of discipleship. Those who truly know Christ, follow him in extending an open invitation to others.

Such a congregation cannot isolate itself into a world of believers and faithfully live out this characteristic. Instead, as the church is reaching out to those in need, it is also extending the invitation of Christ. Rather than being a museum for those who appreciate religious activities, the church is to be a living demonstration of the life and ministry of Jesus. As such, we call others to know and follow Jesus on the basis of common life. We share the following conviction about the nature of the church of Jesus Christ:

> We are closer to the vision of Christ for the church when our common life as believers is focused on inviting others to know and follow the Savior. Evangelism is a corporate endeavor. Our life together is our Gospel tract.
> *The church is a community of invitation.*

In a courtroom setting, witnesses tell others what they have seen or heard. Believers are called to be witnesses by the power of the Holy Spirit. But an invitation goes beyond being a witness. An invitation is a spoken welcome to come to know the one to whom we witness, and in knowing him, to choose to follow him.

Discussion Questions

1. Put into your own words what the "something" is about Jesus in your congregational life that you want others to know and experience.
2. Has anyone ever asked you how to become a Christian? If not, why not? If so, did you know how to reply?
3. How is it important to see the invitation of evangelism as an invitation both to know and to follow Jesus?
4. What can you do in your own congregation to inspire its witness and invitation to others to follow Christ?

CHAPTER THIRTEEN

No More Ice-Cream Parlors

Now when Jesus heard that John had been arrested, he
withdrew to Galilee. He left Nazareth and made his home in
Capernaum by the sea, in the territory of Zebulun and
Naphtali, so that what had been spoken through the prophet
Isaiah might be fulfilled:
*   "Land of Zebulun, land of Naphtali,*
*   on the road by the sea, across the Jordan,*
*   Galilee of the Gentiles—*
*   the people who sat in darkness have seen a great light,*
*   and for those who sat in the region and shadow of death*
*   light has dawned."*
From that time Jesus began to proclaim, "Repent, for the
kingdom of heaven has come near."
*   As he walked by the Sea of Galilee, he saw two brothers,*
Simon, who is called Peter, and Andrew his brother, casting a
net into the sea—for they were fishermen. And he said to

them, *"Follow me, and I will make you fish for people."*
Immediately they left their nets and followed him. As he went
from there, he saw two other brothers, James son of Zebedee
and his brother John, in the boat with their father Zebedee,
mending their nets, and he called them. Immediately they left
the boat and their father, and followed him.

Jesus went throughout Galilee, teaching in their
synagogues and proclaiming the good news of the kingdom
and curing every disease and every sickness among the
people. (Matt. 4:12-23)

Three Kingdom Heralds

Herald No. 1: John the Baptist

In those days John the Baptist appeared in the wilderness of Judea, proclaiming, "Repent, for the kingdom of heaven has come near." (Matt. 3:1-2)

Herald No. 2: Jesus the Christ

Soon afterwards he went on through cities and villages, proclaiming and bringing the good news of the kingdom of God. The twelve were with him, as well as some women. (Luke 8:1-2)

Herald No. 3: The Twelve Disciples

Then Jesus called the twelve together and gave them power and authority over all demons and to cure diseases, and he sent them out to proclaim the kingdom of God and to heal. (Luke 9:1-2)

Ice-Cream Parlors or Restaurants?

Suppose you set a family table for supper. At each place you set out the entire meal of chicken, mashed potatoes, mixed vegetables, and ice cream for dessert. Now you invite everyone to take a seat, including some fairly young children. After grace, you simply invite them to "help yourselves." What part of the meal do you think the children will eat first? It would be an unusual child who didn't go for the ice cream first.

Our contemporary gospel presentations are almost the same. We invite people to receive the gift of forgiveness of sin and eternal life without the invitation to take up their cross and follow Jesus. It begins to feel as if our menu is dessert only, instead of the full course. Like the child, we tend to focus on the dessert and miss the main course. Now dessert is great at the end of a meal, but trying to sustain life on ice cream alone is not wise. In the same way, our message needs to include the full invitation.

Jesus, in the prayer he taught as a pattern for his disciples, encouraged us to pray for God's kingdom to come from heaven to earth (Matt. 6:9-10). In our evangelistic prayers, we encourage people to ask that they be taken from earth to heaven. Aren't we guilty of reversing the emphasis of Jesus? When people come to the end of their life, they will be grateful for the assurance of eternity with the Lord. But in this life, we need to experience the meal's main course—the assurance of Jesus' presence and power here on earth. We need a restaurant, not an ice-cream parlor.

I find myself asking what understanding of evangelism our young people are growing up with in our congregations. Certainly the experiences are varied. Several years ago I had two contrasting experiences within a few weeks. First, I attended a congregation where a mother stood up to share with her congregation the good news that her son, who had grown up in that church, had accepted Christ at a Bible study at a state university where he was attending. The response of the congregation was an awkward silence.

I was curious. So during the break between the worship time and the Sunday school hour, I listened to the conversations. The comments ranged from concern for emotionalism to questions about the correctness of the group. I began to feel that if it didn't happen in their midst, it probably wasn't adequate. I was saddened and felt uncomfortable for the mother, wishing her fellow members could share her desire to rejoice.

A few weeks later, I was in another congregation where a young man stood up to speak. His dress showed that he was directly off the streets. He said he had been walking in the town the previous night when he was stopped by a member of that church, who shared the gospel with him. He had prayed and surrendered his life to Jesus Christ. He started to go on but was interrupted by joyous applause. Immediately I thought of the mother in the other congregation and wondered.

The first young man obviously had more potential for a solid and lasting walk with Christ, but his church was not enthusiastic about it. The second young man had a long way to go to overcome his struggles with sin, but the response of his congregation was a joyous reception. I found myself asking, "What makes one congregation hesitant and suspicious and the other joyful and receptive?" What makes the difference?

I have concluded that congregations who rejoice are congregations at peace with a corporate evangelistic identity. They are a people of God—a community of faith involved in winsomely inviting others to know Christ Jesus as Lord and Savior and to follow him in life. The congregations who are silent are those struggling with unresolved issues and are not totally at peace with the calling they have been given by Jesus himself.

It is my impression that congregations all over North America are experiencing some ambivalence and struggle with evangelism today. We all know that evangelism is important. At the same time, we are uncomfortable both with the message and the method of evangelism commonly associated with revivalism and traditional evangelicalism.

The traditional gospel message has been too much ice cream and not enough main course, and the traditional method of presentation has seemed ineffective.

There is a ditch on both sides of the country road. Swerving too sharply to avoid the ditch on one side may land us in the ditch on the other. I grew up in a mainline Protestant denomination where "evangelism" was synonymous with inviting new people to church on Sunday morning. We never were trained to help someone find a personal relationship with Christ Jesus within a body of believers. We did not really understand that dimension of the task. That was one side of the road.

I joined the Mennonite Church after experiencing a dramatic personal conversion. The first congregation I joined was warmly evangelistic. I felt that I had come home. Later, I began to encounter congregations who had been shaped by an aggressive evangelism associated with revivalism. In order to secure decisions for Christ, preachers had resorted to using fear, guilt, and manipulation of emotions rather than love. The experience of those congregations was the ditch on the other side of the road. Today, some of those same congregations are swerving rapidly toward the practice of evangelism I grew up with. Thus we veer from one ditch to the other.

We have some legitimate doubts about the methods associated with revivalism. Personal evangelism was the work of individuals, and most of the congregation was left out of the picture. "Preaching the gospel" was the role of the evangelist, and it was often understood as emphasizing the guilt of sin and the eternal destiny of the lost without Christ. The solution was for individuals to make a public decision for Christ, after which they were pronounced "saved." While Mennonites participated in such services, most were never really at home with such methods.

This kind of presentation can completely avoid a personal connection between the seeker and those already believers. Carl George of Fuller Seminary says there is a direct correlation between the Holy Spirit's ability to convict unbelievers of their need for a Savior and their relationship with a believing friend. Mennonites would agree. A method of evangelism which does not carry with it the integrity of a personal relationship seems to contradict our vision of church.

Most of us are more comfortable with a "friendship evangelism" approach than a door-to-door method of evangelism or confronting strangers to present the "Roman Road" or "Four Spiritual Laws" booklet. But the problem for most of us as Christians is that we no longer have significant relationships with unbelievers. It is one thing to criticize the methods of revivalism and evangelicalism. It is quite another when we respond by isolating ourselves from any relationships with unbelievers. To avoid the ditch on the one side, we can end up in the ditch on the other side.

Much of what we call evangelism today is merely shuffling saints from one congregation to another. If the message of the gospel is heard only inside the four walls of the church, only our children or the occasional visitor will hear it. The Christian church in our decade is in danger of becoming a community *of* believers, *by* believers, and *for* believers. That is hardly what the church was designed to be, nor was it the vision of the early Anabaptists.

By serving a full-course meal, we can avoid being an ice-cream parlor. But to be a restaurant, we must be open to the public. This is the challenge of the faith community as Jesus envisioned it. Jesus gave an open, personal, deliberate presentation of the kingdom of God. He did not wait for people to come to him, even though some did. He went to them. At the same time, Jesus did not proclaim a message in isolation from a relationship of friendship (John

15:14-15). He presented the message and represented the message. Furthermore, he taught his disciples to do the same.

Thirteenth Keystone

The vision of church we are reaching for is that of a faith community actively involved in inviting others to faith. It is not simply "personal evangelism" where one believer shares with an unbeliever. Mostly, it is the combined efforts of many believers in prayer, love, and caring which draw unbelievers to Jesus. Evangelism is not only the task of the faithful church; it is the identity of the church. It has been said that a church exists for mission as a fire exists for burning.

The vision of church we are reaching for is that of a faith community actively communicating the gospel of the kingdom. The full-course meal is what we invite others to participate in. Rather than simply attempting to get persons tickets to heaven, we are involved in recruiting individuals to form kingdom communities by the creative power of God. As a result, we share the following conviction about the nature of the church of Jesus Christ:

> We are closer to the vision of Christ for the church when inviting others to faith is not just the task of the faith community, but its very identity. The message of the gospel we communicate is not simply about getting to heaven but about getting heaven to earth.
> *The church is a community in invitation.*

This community of faith, rooted in allegiance to Jesus Christ, obedient to his life and teachings, following the way of peace, can truly proclaim the kingdom of God. This community of love, rooted in commitment to one another, cemented through the ministry of servant leaders, and reaching out in compassion to others, can truly welcome others. This is the vision of Christ Jesus for his church.

Discussion Questions

1. How would you describe the Gospel presentation as you have grown up with it? Is it more of an "ice-cream" message or a "full-course meal"?

2. Is your congregation a faith community that is winsomely inviting others to faith in Christ, or does it struggle with such an identity?

3. Do you personally have relationships with unbelievers? Is the lack of such contacts a problem for your congregation? With you?

4. What could your congregation do to mobilize its witness in an authentic and attractive way to those who are outside of Christ and the family of faith?

Built on the Rock

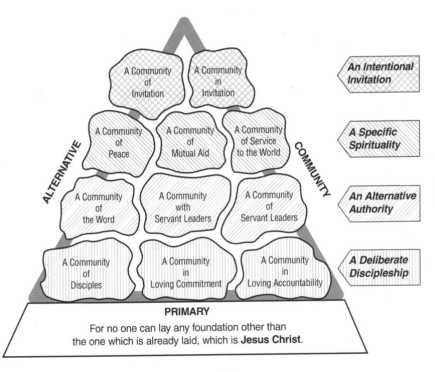

An Intentional Invitation

A Specific Spirituality

An Alternative Authority

A Deliberate Discipleship

A Community of Invitation · A Community in Invitation

A Community of Peace · A Community of Mutual Aid · A Community of Service to the World

A Community of the Word · A Community with Servant Leaders · A Community of Servant Leaders

A Community of Disciples · A Community in Loving Commitment · A Community in Loving Accountability

ALTERNATIVE · COMMUNITY

PRIMARY

For no one can lay any foundation other than the one which is already laid, which is **Jesus Christ**.

Let the Storms Come

Jesus said that the believer who hears his words and puts them into practice is like a wise builder who built his house on the solid foundation of rock. Once completed, it was able to endure rain and wind and flood and still remain standing. As I have worked to put this study into words, I have remembered that encouragement of Christ. If we hear his words and put them into practice, we will be like that wise builder. I can still hear those words.

The view of church I have attempted to describe is the vision which I believe is at the center of our identity as Mennonite Christians. But further, I believe that as we move toward this vision, we move closer to the vision of Jesus himself. More light may be given in the time that remains before the Lord returns, but beginning with this vision, God can reveal more of his purposes.

A Distinctive Definition

What have we discovered of God's purposes? We have found that our understandings of church are shaped by our own experiences and unique vantage points. We realize that our traditional cultural views of church do not always agree with the life and teachings of Jesus. We also have recognized that the view of church retained within the Mennonite community is significantly different from those oriented around the sacraments or the preaching ministry. We have focused on a definition of church as a primary, alternative, faith community.

A Deliberate Discipleship

To become such a faith community means a different view of conversion. A genuine turning to the Lord moves through the experience of a new birth into a lifelong commitment of faithfulness to Christ. The church must be a community of disciples. Additionally, becoming such a community requires a commitment to loving relationships with one another. We discover we cannot be disciples alone; we need one another to live the Christian life. This requires a commitment to each other to be the sisters and brothers that God wants us to be. We begin to recognize that the church is a committed community. This is a vision of church rooted in covenant—God's commitment to us, our commitment to God, and our mutual covenant with each other before God.

An Alternative Authority

To become such a faith community means we have an alternative vision of authority. First of all, the Scriptures are authoritative for us because they reveal the intention of God for how we should live. To become such a faith community, we must approach the Scriptures with a readiness to obey. Additionally, we have a different view of leadership authority within the congregation. Rather than a pastoral elite, we understand leadership as a part of the congregation. What makes pastors different from other believers is their task and gifting, not their position. Leaders are given authority by the congregation to assemble individual believers into a congregation. In turn, pastors lead out of a sense of partnership with the congregation as together they attempt to do the work of God.

A Specific Spirituality

To become such a faith community also means we need a specific view of spirituality. Rather than countering the violence of this age with further violence, we believe the Spirit of Jesus is the spirit of love. As such, it turns the other cheek, returns good for evil, and seeks to win the enemy with acts of love. To be filled with the Spirit means, in part, to be filled with the character of Jesus; this is contrary to the violent spirit of this age. To be such a community of faith, we respond with compassion to those in need. The Spirit of Jesus can not be domesticated and confined to the Christian community. As we are led by the Spirit, we are involved in the needs of the world.

An Intentional Invitation

To become such a faith community finally means being a people of invitation. Evangelism must not be simply the task of a few individual believers but of the entire congregation. In fact, it is not just the task of the faith community but its very identity. The church is a people of invitation. Hence, we must be clear about the message and the method. The message is an invitation to experience and extend the kingdom of God on earth. The method is through relationships of love and integrity. The church is both a community of invitation and a community in invitation.

My prayer is that this vision of church will help you understand the vision at the heart of the Mennonite faith community. I pray that in understanding it better, you will conclude with me that this is the way of Jesus. In understanding this vision, may you give your all to make it a reality, to the glory of God. Then we can say: Let the storms come; we are building on the Rock!

Notes

1. *Laetentur Coeli* (Let the heavens rejoice), "Decree of the Council of Florence," 1439. In *New Catholic Encyclopedia* (New York: McGraw Hill, 1967), 11:779.

2. Martin Luther, "Against the Roman Papacy, an Institution of the Devil." In *Luther's Works*, ed. by Eric W. Gritch (Philadelphia: Fortress Press, 1966), 41:314.

3. Pilgram Marpeck, "The Admonition of 1542." In *The Writings of Pilgram Marpeck*, trans. and ed. by William Klassen and Walter Klaassen (Scottdale, Pa.: Herald Press, 1978), 230.

4. Pope Pius XII, "Mediator Dei," 66. In *Acta Apostolicae Sedis, Commentarium Officiale* (Rome: Libreria Editrice Vaticana, 1947), 39:521-595.

5. Martin Luther and Philipp Melanchthon, "Augsburg Confession, Article VIII: Of the Church." In *The Book of Concord*, trans. and ed. by Theodore G. Tappert (Philadelphia: Fortress Press, 1959), 32.

6. Robert Stupperich, *Die Schriften Bernhard Rothmann* (Münster i. Westfalen: Aschendorffsche Verlagsbuchhandlung, 1970), 241.

7. Balthasar Hubmaier, "The Sum of a Christian Life." In *Quellen zur Geschichte der Täufer in der Schweiz, 2. Band: Ostschweiz,*

ed. by Heinold Fast (Zurich: Theologisher Verlag, 1973), 111-112.

8. Melchior Hoffman, "Ordinance of God," 1530. In *Spiritual and Anabaptist Writers*, ed. by George H. Williams and A. M. Mergal (Philadelphia: Westminster Press, 1957), 186-188.

9. Menno Simons, "Foundations," 1539. In *The Complete Writings of Menno Simons*, trans. by Leonard Verduin, ed. by J. C. Wenger (Scottdale, Pa.: Herald Press, 1956), 125.

10. Hans Denck, "The Contention That Scripture Says," 1526. In *Schriften*, 2. Teil: *Religiöse Schriften*, ed. by Walter Fellmann (Gütersloh: C. Bertelsmann Verlag, 1956), 45, 50.

11. Michael Sattler, "Letter to the Church at Horb," 1527. In *The Legacy of Michael Sattler*, trans. and ed. by John H. Yoder (Scottdale, Pa.: Herald Press, 1973), 59.

12. Ulrich Stadler, "Cherished Instructions," about 1537. In *Spiritual and Anabaptist Writers*, 278.

13. Dirk Philips, "Refutation of Two Letters of Sebastian Franck," about 1563. In *Enchiridion*, trans. by A. B. Kolb (Aylmer, Ont.: Pathway Publishing Corp., 1966). English trans. rev. by Walter Klaassen, based on *Der Geshriften van Dirk Philipsz, Bibliotheca Reformatoria Neerlandica*, ed. by S. Cramer and F. Pijper (Nijhoff, Netherlands, 1914), 10:206.

14. Bernhard Rothmann, "Restitution," 1534. In *Quellen zur Geschichte der Täufer,* 5. Band: *Bayern,* 2. *Abteilung,* ed. by Karl Schornbaum (Gütersloh: C. Bertelsmann Verlag, 1951), 22.

15. Michael Sattler, "Schleitheim Confession," 1527. In *The Legacy of Michael Sattler,* 38-39.

16. Hans Hotz, "Bern Colloquy," 1538. In *Quellen zur Geschichte der Täufer in der Schweiz,* 4. Band: *Drei Täufergespräche,* ed. by Martin Haas (Zurich: Theologisher Verlag, 1974), 287-288.

17. Peter Riedemann, "Concerning Election," 1542. In *Account of Our Religion, Doctrine and Faith* (London: Hodder and Stoughton, and Rifton, N.Y.: Plough Publishing, 1950), 81.

18. Samuel Geiser, "An Ancient Anabaptist Witness for Nonresistance, 1529," *Mennonite Quarterly Review* 25 (Jan. 1951): 66-69, 72.

19. Peter Riedemann, "Concerning the Making of Swords,"

1542. In *Account of Our Religion, Doctrine and Faith,* 111-112.

20. Menno Simons, "Reply to False Accusations," 1552. In *The Complete Writings of Menno Simons,* 554.

21. Ronald Sider, "God's People Reconciling." In *Proceedings, Mennonite World Conference, XI Assembly, Strasbourg, 1984* (Lombard, Ill.: Mennonite World Conference, 1984), 252.

22. Peter Riedemann, "Concerning Warfare," 1542. In *Account of Our Religion, Doctrine and Faith,* 109.

23. Ulrich Stadler, "Cherished Instructions," about 1537. In *Spiritual and Anabaptist Writers,* 284.

24. Balthasar Hubmaier, "Conversation on Zwingli's Book on Baptism," 1526. In *The Writings of Balthasar Hubmaier,* collected and photographed by W. O. Lewis, trans. and ed. by George D. Davidson, English trans. rev. by Walter Klaassen (microfilm at Conrad Grebel College, Waterloo, Ont., 1939), 2:157.

25. Dirk Philips, "The Evangelical Ban and Shunning," 1602. In *Enchiridion,* 391-393.

26. Menno Simons, "Why I Do Not Cease Teaching and Writing," 1539. In *The Complete Writings of Menno* Simons, 307.

27. Menno Simons, "Why I Do Not Cease Teaching and Writing." In *The Complete Writings of Menno Simons,* 303.

28. Menno Simons, "Why I Do Not Cease Teaching and Writing." In *The Complete Writings of Menno Simons,* 304.

29. Menno Simons, "Why I Do Not Cease Teaching and Writing." In *The Complete Writings of Menno Simons,* 306-307.

Resources

(Herald Press books unless otherwise noted)

Barrett, Lois. *Building the House Church.* 1986.

Becker, Palmer. *Called to Care: A Training Manual for Small Group Leaders.* 1993.

_____. *Called to Equip: A Training and Resource Manual for Pastors.* 1993.

Bender, H. S. *These Are My People.* 1962.

_____. Anabaptist Vision. 1944.

_____. "Church." In *The Mennonite Encyclopedia*, 1:594-598. Vols. 1-4, ed. by C. Krahn et al., 1955-59.

Birkey, Del. *The House Church: A Model for Renewing the Church.* 1988.

Bontrager, G. Edwin, and Nathan D. Showalter. *It Can Happen Today! Principles of Church Growth from the Book of Acts.* 1986.

Byler, Dennis. *Making War and Making Peace: Why Some Christians Fight and Some Don't.* 1989.

Caes, David. *Caring for the Least of These.* 1992.

Drescher, John M. *Why I Am a Conscientious Objecter.* 1982.

Durnbaugh, Donald. *The Believers' Church.* 1985.

Dyck, Cornelius J. *An Introduction to Mennonite History: A Popular History of the Anabaptists and the Mennonites.* Rev. 3d ed., 1993.

_____. "Church, Doctrine of." In *The Mennonite Encyclopedia*, 5:150-152. Vol. 5 ed. by C. J. Dyck et al. 1990.

_____. *Spiritual Life in Anabaptism.* 1995.

Gwyn, Douglas, et al. *A Declaration on Peace: In God's People the World's Renewal Has Begun.* 1990.

Halteman, James. *The Clashing Worlds of Economics and Faith.* 1995.

Harder, Leland. *Doors to Lock and Doors to Open: The Discerning People of God.* 1993.

Hershberger, Guy F., ed. *The Recovery of the Anabaptist Vision.* 1957.

Hostetler, John A. *An invitation to Faith.* 1957.

Jeschke, Marlin. *Discipling in the Church: Recovering a Ministry of the Gospel.* Rev. expanded ed., 1988.

Klaassen, Walter. *Anabaptism in Outline: Selected Primary Sources.* 1981.

_____. *Anabaptism: Neither Catholic nor Protestant.* Waterloo: Conrad Press, 1973.

Klassen, Randolph J. *Jesus' Word, Jesus' Way.* 1992.

Kraus, C. Norman. *The Community of the Spirit: How the Church Is in the World.* 1993.

Littell, Franklin H. *The Origins of Sectarian Protestantism: A Study of the Anabaptist View of the Church.* New York: Macmillan, 1964.

Loewen, Harry, and Steven Nolt, with Carol Duerkson and Elwood Yoder. *Through Fire and Water: An Overview of Mennonite History.* 1995.

Marshall, Jay W. *The Ten Commandments and Christian Community.* 1995.

Mummert, J. Ronald, with Jeff Bach. *Refugee Ministry in the Local Congregation.* 1992.

Schmitt, Abraham and Dorothy. *When a Congregation Cares: A New Approach to Crisis Ministries.* 1984.

Shenk, David W., and Ervin R. Stutzman. *Creating Communities of the Kingdom: New Testament Models of Church Planting.* 1988.

Shenk, David W. *God's Call to Mission.* 1994.

Shenk, Wilbert R. *The Church in Mission.* 1984.

Sider, Ronald J. *Christ and Violence.* 1979.

Smith, Christian. *Going to the Root: Nine Proposals for Radical Church Renewal.* 1992.

Smith, Luther E., Jr. *Intimacy and Mission: Intentional Community as Crucible for Radical Discipleship*, 1994.

Steiner, Susan Clemmer. *Joining the Army That Sheds No Blood.* 1982.

Stutzman, Ervin R. *Welcome! A Biblical and Practical Guide to Receiving New Members.* 1990.

Weaver, J. Denny. *Becoming Anabaptist.* 1987.

Wenger, A. Grace, and Dave and Neta Jackson. *Witness: Empowering the Church Through Worship, Community, and Mission.* 1989.

Wenger, J. C. *What Mennonites Believe.* Rev. ed., 1991.

_____. *The Family of Faith.* 1981.

Yoder, John H. *Nevertheless: The Varieties and Shortcomings of Religious Pacifism.* Rev. 3d ed., 1992.

_____. *What Would You Do [if a violent person threatened to harm a loved one]? A Serious Answer to a Standard Question.* Expanded ed., 1992.

Zunkel, C. Wayne. *Church Growth Under Fire.* 1987.

p. 36. God said to a person, you are incompatible .... and I don't change

The Author

Wally Fahrer—from his experience as a pastor, church planter, missionary, and conference minister—brings a unique perspective to the important issue of church identity. He is a Mennonite by choice, having become one as an adult, along with his wife. Subsequently he was called to ministry in the congregation they joined. Fahrer completed his seminary training at Associated Mennonite Biblical Seminary, Elkhart, Indiana, and has served in congregations in the USA and England.

For five years Fahrer was Minister of Missions for the Indiana-Michigan Mennonite Conference and thus overseeing several emerging Mennonite congregations. He encouraged church planters to develop Anabaptist-Mennonite congregations, both in name and character. Out of that ministry, this book has been written.

Fahrer was born in Wahoo, Nebraska, and raised in the rural Kansas community of Lindsborg. He is married to Susan Engelbrecht of suburban Chicago, and they have three children, Rebecca, Bethany, and David.

In 1993 Fahrer returned to London, England, as Overseas Missionary, associated with the Mennonite Board of Missions. There the Fahrers work with an independent Christian congregation, Cholmeley Evangelical Church, where Wally has primary pastoral responsibility as part of the leadership team.